Is God Saying
HE'S THE ONE?

*Hearing from Heaven
About That Man in Your Life*

SUSAN ROHRER

Infinite Arts Media

IS GOD SAYING HE'S THE ONE?
HEARING FROM HEAVEN
ABOUT THAT MAN IN YOUR LIFE
Written by Susan Rohrer

Kindly direct all professional inquiries via:
InfiniteArtsMgmt@gmail.com

Readers may contact author at:
shelfari.com/susanrohrer

Excepting brief excerpts for review purposes, no part of this book may be reproduced or used in any form without written permission from the author. Except as otherwise noted, all Scripture quotations taken from the New American Standard Bible®, Copyright © 1960, 1962, 1963, 1968, 1971, 1972, 1973, 1975, 1977, 1995 by The Lockman Foundation Used by permission. (www.Lockman.org)

Scripture quotations noted as ASV are from THE HOLY BIBLE: American Standard Version which is in the public domain worldwide.

Cover Image: piyaphantawong / FreeDigitalPhotos.net

Author photo by Jean-Louis Darville (with permission)

Copyright © 2012, Susan Rohrer, all rights reserved.

Published in the United States of America

First Edition 2012

"My sheep hear My voice, and I know them, and they follow Me."

John 10:27

Contents

ONE 9
Hearing from Heaven

TWO 19
Who's That Talking?

THREE 47
Defining the Relationship

FOUR 65
Things God Definitely Said

FIVE 91
How God Helps Sort the Laundry

SIX 113
Kicking the Best Friend Habit

SEVEN 135
Healing for the Heartsick

EIGHT 159
How to Know if He's The One

NINE 175
The Wedding Singer

ABOUT THE AUTHOR 185

To every woman who longs to hear
the voice of her beloved.

ONE

Hearing from Heaven

"Out of the heavens He let you hear His voice..."

Deuteronomy 4:36

It was a picture perfect day for a wedding. The church was idyllic. I'll never forget the sight of my friend walking down the aisle in that exquisite dress. She couldn't have looked more beautiful. As she glided past the pew where I was seated—her gaze fixed on her betrothed—a still, small voice whispered to me:

This will not end well.

I didn't know the groom at all. We'd never had a single conversation. And yet, as my friend neared him at the altar, suddenly, everything in me realized that he was *not* The One for her.

I felt sick to my stomach.

It was nothing short of ominous when the minister asked if anyone knew a reason why the couple should not be married. A hush fell over the sanctuary as time was allowed for any objections. Inside, I screamed the only *"I do"* that should have been said on that day.

Still, there had been no heaven-sent instruction to interfere. I was also sure that any attempt of mine to stop the wedding would have been futile. So, I sat in troubled silence as the ceremony continued.

Indeed, it wasn't long before my friend found herself in the midst of a terrible divorce. She had chosen to marry that man in her life, and the consequences had been nearly catastrophic.

There are some days that are burned in our memories. We recall those times in vivid detail. Those pivotal moments at that particular wedding are like that for me. In His grace, the Lord used it to teach me an important lesson.

It's not that I've heard anything like that at a wedding-in-progress since. But over the years, God has given me many opportunities to counsel other women concerning just what He has to say about the men in their lives. This experience reminds me not to take their questions lightly.

Over the course of this book, I'll share some true stories. With the exception of certain family members and authors whose books I recommend, the names have been changed to protect the privacy of those involved. Some stories are cautionary and others are joyful. I hope that all of them will lend a hand to every reader who asks her heavenly Father for guidance about that man in her life.

Not long ago, someone asked me why I was writing this particular book. She knew that there was no bolt from the blue when I married so young, without a voice from heaven to advise me.

Though the Bible says believers will hear God's voice, I hadn't had much experience with that by the time of my wedding. The closest thing I had to a confirmation was learning that my unknown future husband had become a believer during the exact month when I had started praying for him. This was long before I knew who he was. I was still a high school senior at the time. He was a freshman in college. I hadn't even decided on that particular school where we'd ultimately meet. But God went before me and answered that prayer, redeeming the man who became The One for me.

It was well into my first year of marriage that I began to experience what the Bible says will be true of God's sheep. I heard His voice. It was so clear that I turned and looked over my right shoulder to see if anyone was there. There was no mistaking the gentle authority with which He spoke, calling me to make movies for Him. Just like the Bible says sheep will, I recognized His voice and I purposed to follow His direction.

Over the years, as God brought those first words to fulfillment in my life in amazing ways, I longed to hear His voice and more. Hearing from Him with such clarity was far from a regular occurrence, but my desire to hear that sweet sound grew into a frequent subject of study and prayer. Little did I know that God would answer my prayer in the middle of a friend's wedding, or that He had so much to say about the men in our lives. I began to realize how crucial it is to consult Him about this important choice.

I'll be clear with you from the start that I'm not a professional counselor. I'm not ordained, or in any kind of official church leadership. But over the years, there have been many times when God has directed me to come alongside specific women who are struggling with the question this book poses: *Is God Saying He's The One?*

Volumes could be written on the subject of discerning God's voice. Many volumes have been, most notably the Bible. As spectacular as it may seem, God's voice is a voice we were created to hear.

If you've read my first book, *THE HOLY SPIRIT: Amazing Power for Everyday People*, then you know how firmly I believe that God still speaks to those who listen. But does the Holy Spirit go beyond general communication to guidance about the specific details of our lives, even so far as to speak to the identity of a woman's future husband?

Of all the queries I field about hearing from heaven, among the most regular is the question I heard from an out-of-state friend, Rachel. She had just been reading about hearing God's voice in my first book. It was something Rachel said she'd been wrestling with lately. She was wondering whether or not she was hearing from God about a particular man from her church. We'll call him Keith.

Rachel told me that Keith was a devoted believer. She said they were like best friends. But whenever she asked God to speak to her about her marital future, all she heard was *"Not now."* The voice was always immediate, gentle, and reassuring. Each time she inquired, over and over, there were only those two words. So Rachel posed that question so many have asked, a question you may have today:

"How do I know if God is telling me that he's The One?"

Maybe I hear women asking about men more often than the other way around because, by far, most of my confidants are women. So, I'll start by acknowledging that everything I say here could just as easily be flipped to apply to the other gender.

Though many men also want to hear from God on this subject—far more often than not—this question comes to me from a single woman, a believer not presently in a romantic relationship, but highly desirous of one.

Usually, there is a specific object of this woman's affections. Often, it's a guy who is already a friend—someone who treats her with some level of recognition, even best friend-like familiarity. The problem is he hasn't pursued her romantically or admitted to seeing her in *that way* yet.

She waits, nurturing the relationship. She hopes for this friendship to shift into an intentional gear. She watches closely for signals that what she longs for is, indeed, coming. Circumstances seem to confirm.

Affection grows to longing. She confides in her closest friends, enlisting them in prayer. She regularly petitions the Almighty about this man, inquiring with all her heart: *"Are you saying he's The One?"*

"Delight yourself in the Lord; and He will give you the desires of your heart."
Psalm 37:4

In light of this promise that the Lord will give us the desires of our hearts if we will first delight ourselves in Him, it doesn't seem unreasonable to ask God about what can be one of the deepest desires of our hearts: to be known and loved by another person, a man of God's own choosing.

Yes, if God is our greatest delight, He will give us as much of Himself as we desire. But there's also plenty of room in that promise to allow that God might speak to a person's desire for a spouse. After all, He weighed in from the very beginning that it wasn't good for *people* to be alone, didn't He?

You may have noticed that I just italicized the word *people*. It's not that I was adapting the biblical text in an effort to be politically correct. I did it because I hope women will be encouraged to discover that the original Hebrew word commonly translated as *man* in Genesis 2:18 doesn't exclusively refer to guys. It translates to include all humans—that means any person—male or female.

So, even though God was considering Adam's state when it's translated that God said it wasn't good for *man* to be alone, the word *man* was used in a *humankind* sense that includes men and women. You know how Adam's condition was used to represent all humans in many other Scriptural references? You can think of it kind of like that. Also in this verse, when it says it's "not good" to be alone, the word for *good* embraces the masculine as well as the feminine.

Stop for a moment and think about this.

From the very beginning, God observed the deep need men and women have for each other. The creation of womankind was not an afterthought. It didn't take our omniscient God by surprise that Adam would need a mate. This wasn't a holy oops. God had already created every kind of animal, implicitly including males and females as He blessed them, saying that they should be fruitful and multiply.

God knew before He formed Adam from the dust, before He breathed life into his nostrils, that Eve would also be created to become Adam's wife. He even gave Adam time alone in the garden to name and observe the animals with their mates, perhaps to generate a yearning in Adam for the missing human counterpart God knew was to come.

Anyone who has ever spent time alone understands the longing for relationship it can prompt. Just as hunger prompts us to eat and thirst make us want something to drink, so time without committed companionship draws us to desire each other.

If you read through the opening chapters of Genesis, you'll see that until the first human being was created, God had surveyed what He'd made and declared that it was all good. It was not until after God had created both Adam and Eve that God emphasized His satisfaction by gazing at everything that He had made and pronouncing that it was *very* good.

In fact, the very first thing God deemed as *not* good was for a human being to be alone. This reveals our heavenly Father's very observant eye and compassionate heart for singles. It tells us that He indeed speaks to our need for relationship, right from the dawn of time.

Though I began this book as a way to answer Rachel, I hope it will be meaningful to you. If Rachel's question also burns in your heart, would you stop and say a quick prayer?

Before you read any more, take some quiet time to invite the Lord to go with you on this personal journey of faith. You can use your own words if you want. You can use the prayer I've provided for you on the next page. Just take the time to sit with the Lord, and mean every word that you say.

Father in heaven,

You are so great and I am so unworthy. But I thank You that You call me Your daughter. It's amazing to think about what Jesus said, that His sheep would hear His voice.

I know I'm just one of many sheep in Your pasture, but I want to hear You, just like Jesus said I would. Help me to recognize when it's You speaking. Teach me the difference between Your voice and any other voices I may hear.

I open my ears to hear You, Lord, whatever You have to say. I welcome You to share Your truth with me, even if it's not something I want to hear.

Every time I open this book to read, I invite the Holy Spirit to speak to me. Confirm Yourself to me through Scripture and godly counsel. Help me to be sure of Your guidance in my specific situation.

No matter what, I want Your very best for me. No matter what, I am grateful to hear from You.

Speak, Lord.
Your servant is listening.

TWO

Who's That Talking?

> *"And let two or three prophets speak, and let the others pass judgment...and the spirits of the prophets are subject to the prophets; for God is not a God of confusion, but of peace..."*
>
> *I Corinthians 14:29,32–33*

It might strike some as odd to kick off this chapter with a passage about prophecy. But then again, this is more than a book about naturally deducing who might be The One in our lives. It's about hearing what God has to say on the subject. That's why I suggested to Rachel that she should read about prophetic communication as she sought counsel about that *"Not now"* she was hearing.

This book is for women of faith, those who long to know if their match is truly being made in heaven. It's for women like Rachel who long to hear the voice of God and wonder if they have. It's for those times when the incredible appears to be happening—when God seems to disclose the identity of that special man a woman will come to marry. It's for women like my friend, Kelly, who was already accustomed to hearing from heaven.

Kelly was born a pastor's daughter. From the time she learned to string words together, she would talk to God. Kelly's mom said she'd hear Kelly chattering away in another room and would ask who was at the other end of the conversation.

"God," little Kelly would say.

"Well, is He saying anything back?" her mom used to inquire.

"Yep!" Kelly would chirp in reply.

Oh, for the faith of a little child! Kelly simply believed the Bible when it said that God's sheep would hear His voice, and that young and old would hear from heaven in visions and dreams.

As Kelly grew to womanhood, so did her faith. Still, she continued to interact with God. As guys began to notice her, she recalls receiving a brief vision of a man. He was dressed in such a way that Kelly thought he might be a producer in the entertainment industry. She noticed his height as well as the color of his hair and beard. Mostly, she was struck with his shining eyes.

As Kelly mulled the picture over, she thought, *"He looks nice. Comfortable. Like the sort of guy I might enjoy being with."* By then, Kelly was mature enough in her faith to acknowledge the possibility that this picture could have been just her imagination, longing to fill in the romantic blank in her life. On the other hand, if it were from God, she knew it would come to pass. Not wanting to presume anything beyond the simple picture she saw, Kelly tucked it away loosely in her memory and didn't compare the guys she dated to it.

In time, Kelly met Tim at her workplace. As handsome as he was personable, Tim attracted quite a bit of female attention. Though Kelly was friendly with Tim, she wasn't particularly drawn to him at first. However, one day, Tim seemed to show a special interest in her. Soon afterward, Kelly said she heard, *"Love Tim. Love Timothy."* Suddenly, something blossomed in Kelly's heart for Tim, given what she embraced as encouragement from God.

Maybe you've heard a still, small voice yourself. It may have been more like thunder. Perhaps you received an unconfirmed prophetic word delivered by another believer. An interested man may claim to have heard from God about you. You may be wondering if it was God who visited you in that dream about marrying that special guy. You might be curious to know just who's been posting those little signs you've noticed. Maybe it's more of a subtle leading you feel, as if your heavenly Father keeps pointing you in a certain man's direction. These are all scriptural ways God has been known to communicate with His people, but the question is always:

Was it really God?

Just as Kelly believed, Jesus said that His sheep would hear His voice. When we actually do, we experience something of the prophetic—as living and active words from God bubble up like a fountain. That's what the word *prophecy* means. It's God's refreshing spring of grace to His people.

Prophetic words exhort, encourage, and console us about things present as well as things to come (I Corinthians 14:3). It was prophetic when God's angel encouraged Joseph to take Mary as his wife in Matthew 1:20, and it's just as prophetic if and when God truly speaks to this choice today.

Did the words Kelly heard about Tim prove to be prophetic of her marital future?

No. We laugh about it now. But at the time, it caused quite a bit of heartache and confusion. You see, Kelly fell hard for Tim after embracing those words. With each passing day, she became more invested in the hope that he was The One for her.

Since Kelly recognized the name *Timothy* from the Bible, she scoured scriptural texts under that name for insight. Kelly looked forward to interactions with Tim, but for some reason found that she was completely unable to have a normal conversation when she saw him. No matter how she tried, she could hardly put two words together in his presence.

It was not that she held Tim up to the standard of the vision she'd seen. If she had, she would have noticed that Tim's hair and eye coloring were not a match. She might have also realized that she was anything but comfortable with Tim, the way she had been with the man in the picture. Still, Kelly hung onto those words she'd thought she'd heard, that seeming instruction to give Tim her heart. It was an easy mistake to make, especially since Kelly was still growing in her understanding about how to best discern and confirm God's voice.

Before long, the secret that Kelly had an unnamed crush leaked out. It became a comedy of errors when another co-worker mistakenly thought that *he* was the object of her affections. Enter yet another charming fellow who began to pursue Kelly unwittingly. He was a congenial sort, but by then Kelly was so enamored with Tim that she refused to give the pursuer a chance. Other men asked Kelly out and she turned every one of them down, preferring to wait for Tim.

Nothing about this was working. Nothing confirmed that those words really were from God. It was like a bad TV rom-com where the heroine winds up alone, comforting herself with a gallon of Rocky Road and way too many cats.

At long last, Kelly sought counsel with her father, since he was also a pastor. When she said how convinced she was that God had said Tim was The One, her dad wasn't so sure. While he agreed that Tim was a great guy, he didn't think Tim was as right for Kelly as she thought he was.

Soon, Kelly consulted another a believer who stressed how easily we can be deceived when it comes to matters of the heart, even if we've heard God's prophetic voice accurately about other things. These back-to-back cautions encouraged Kelly to open herself to the possibility that it might not have been God who said that Tim was The One.

The icing on this counseling cake came quickly, when two women approached Kelly separately within a single day. Both of these sisters were convinced that God had said *the same man* was The One for them. Knowing that couldn't have been true helped Kelly see the truth about herself, that she, too, had been mistaken. When Kelly prayed about this, God gave her a sweetly personal vision. Through it, He showed Kelly that He was closing the door on this episode in her life. He didn't chide her for misunderstanding. He didn't say she'd never marry, but He gently made it clear that Tim would not be The One for her.

Was God finished with Kelly's love story? Not by a long shot, but I'll tell you more about that later.

Keeping Prophecy in Perspective

It's always tempting to be most interested in hearing from God about our own lives. Let's admit that. So, we should all regularly remind ourselves that the primary role of the spiritual gift of prophecy is to edify *others* within the body of Christ.

In context, Paul's instructions speak to how prophecy should function as a service to the body in corporate church gatherings. But even when it's that gentle whispering within the privacy of a believer's spirit (and maybe especially so), there is real wisdom in closely examining anything we believe we're hearing from God. This is true whether a word comes directly to us or if it's delivered through another person. That way, confirming Scripture and counsel can help to alleviate confusion about what God is and isn't saying.

If a voice speaks to you about your love life, ask yourself: does what I'm hearing about this man line up with what has been well established as God's spoken truth of the Bible? Any message that is really from heaven will stand up to the test of Scripture. It will also pass muster with godly counsel.

Paul's instructions about submitting prophetic words to the discerning ears of other witnesses is echoed in his second letter to the Corinthian church:

> *"At the mouth of two witnesses or three shall every word be established."*
> *II Corinthians 13:1 ASV*

By now, some might be saying, "You can't be serious. You don't really expect me to confide my intimate exchanges with God with anyone else, especially when it comes to that man in my life."

Sure enough, some might say it's making too big a deal of it, but think about it. Who we are to marry is one of the most important decisions we can make in our lives. This is no small stakes issue. So, if we believe God may be saying that a particular man is The One, it qualifies as a word that should be confirmed by two or three witnesses. We should wait and get that confirmation before we allow the idea to take root in our hearts that it was God who said it.

As important as it is for believers to embrace true prophetic communication from the Almighty, it's just as vital to follow each of the Bible's directives concerning all forms of prophecy. That way, we can weed out those words that may seem to be from God, but aren't.

For those who'd like to read more about the gift of prophecy in much greater detail as Rachel did, there are chapters on aural prophecy as well as prophetic communiqués via visions and dreams in my book, *THE HOLY SPIRIT: Amazing Power for Everyday People*. But, for the more specific purposes of this book, suffice it to say that whether a message is of a verbal or visionary variety, it should be carefully examined for consistency with what the Bible has to say. It should also be submitted to the judgment of godly counsel.

Need a prophetic counselor? Look for mature believers in your church or circle of faith, those who have a history of accurately hearing from God in this way. Make sure that anyone you approach for counsel is reasonably accessible to you. It helps if your counselors know you or have a place of respect in your life. This is especially important when we seek counsel about any voice that speaks to what we'd like to hear, like the identity of a desired future spouse.

Okay. I can hear some of you moaning out there. I can see some shaking their heads and thinking—*no way I'd submit this to anyone else for counsel!* But before preemptively jettisoning this very biblical practice, remember that the Bible exhorts us to do this for our good. Prophetic counsel can support and encourage us if the words we've heard are confirmed as true. Conversely, godly counselors can offer correction and consolation if the words we've heard are discerned as having come from our own heart's desires. It's a win-win.

We may hesitate to consult counselors out of shyness or embarrassment. We may resist hearing what's contrary to our hopes. We may be intimidated by the idea of inquiring of those who prophesy, fearful of what they'll think of us. Still, consider what Solomon had to say about seeking godly counsel:

> *"Where there is no guidance, the people fall, but in abundance of counselors there is great victory."*
>
> *Proverbs 11:14*

Laying your whole heart and spirit bare in the company of biblical counselors may seem anything but safe to you. It might sound downright terrifying. Hesitation to seek counsel about what we believe we've heard from God definitely has its roots sunk deep into fear.

We hold our private ground, afraid they'll be wrong. We're even more terror-struck at the chance of being wrong ourselves (translation: pride). We're incredibly reluctant to confront the possibility that we haven't heard from God at all.

Be encouraged, Sisters. Think of how many times God accompanies His true messages with the instruction to *"fear not."* If you fear the very mode of confirmation God outlines for us in Scripture, guess where that fear is coming from. (Hint: it's not from God.)

There really is safety in receiving godly counsel about this question. It saves us from veering off course and sets our feet on a secure path. Either way it goes, it gives us the opportunity to enlist our counselors in prayer for us, the way I prayed for Rachel after she sought counsel from me.

The fact is that independent counselors can be more objective about these things than we can. They can attune their ears to God without the voice of a human heart's desires competing for an audience, the way it does when we listen to God for direction concerning our own lives or for those closest to us. They can help us sort through it when we've gone beyond correctly hearing a general promise of a future marriage to an incorrect assumption about who the groom will be.

As Paul recorded in I Corinthians 13:9, we both know and prophesy only in part. More than once I've heard prophecy that a particular woman would come to be a bride. Repeatedly, I've seen the elated woman apply that prophetic word or vision to a specific man, only to be devastated when her added assumption of the groom's identity proved to be false. Then, years later, I've seen what God actually promised come to be in astounding detail, tracking with the part that was truly prophetic.

Rachel was wise to seek counsel about the *"Not now"* she heard. If God really did say it, it could have still been so easy to fall into the error of adding onto it. She could have expanded those two words to apply to Keith when they just as easily could have indicated a delay in marriage to someone yet to be revealed.

On the other hand, if that *"Not now"* happened to be the voice of Rachel's heart's desire talking, it would be important to know that, too. Sometimes our hearts give us a *"Not now"* to justify hanging onto hope that a particular man will come around when we should be moving on with life.

Time Will Tell

The definitive answer to whether or not a word, vision, or dream was indeed prophetic may take a while to come.

Meet Anna. Years ago, Anna had a very striking dream. In this dream, she saw a compelling man she had never met before. His name was Alexander. Though Anna didn't think much more about Alexander after relating the dream, her sisters were more imaginative about just who this mysterious man in her dream might come to be.

I remember sitting with a young man, Jon, at a family wedding reception. He told me how he had met Anna in college. Excitedly, he shared just how special Anna had become to him. I knew that Jon had made the decision back in his teens that he wasn't interested in recreational dating. Instead, he had just prayed that God would lead him straight to the woman he was to marry. So, I asked Jon if he thought Anna was The One. A confident smile crossed Jon's face as he nodded. Indeed, he did.

Naturally, I was all ears, eager to hear more. Jon related the story of how he'd become friends with

Anna in classes together. In a similar field of study, they had very compatible life goals and spiritual commitments.

After a long while, Jon had asked Anna if she would be willing to take some dedicated time to pray about dating him, understanding that he'd want it to be an intentional relationship. So, the two of them took a block of time separately to seek the Lord about each other.

Jon told me how, in prayer, both Anna and he had sensed that God would bless their relationship. Both sensed a *"yes"* from their heavenly Father. It was only after they compared notes and agreed to move forward as a couple that Anna first learned what Jon's middle name is:

Alexander.

What a wonderful confirmation that was! Anna hadn't resisted Jon because of the dream, but both the *"yes"* and the dream stood in independent agreement. When Anna and Jon Alexander married after graduation, it was a truly joyful occasion. Through that dream, God had confirmed that Jon was The One for Anna, but He had spoken it in a mystery that would unravel in due time.

There are those who ask why God would give a prophetic dream or word to a woman long before He knows it will come to pass. They protest that we shouldn't have to wait for fulfillment as long as Anna did. But God knows what He's doing when He lovingly shows us these pieces of what's to come. Sometimes, it's just about teaching us faith, to believe in what we can't see yet.

God also knows when a painful breakup is ahead. He knows when a man you may have set your hopes on simply won't respond to you. In a number of ways, those in-part prophecies are expressions of His tender mercies:

- They give us a hope to hang onto as we weather broken-heartedness.

- They encourage us to move on with faith in our Father's great concern for us, through hardship and loneliness.

- They multiply our gratitude to God when they, in fact, come to pass.

Hearing Anna's story may prompt many to start petitioning heaven for a name. I'll emphasize that Anna was not doing that when God chose to give the name *Alexander* to her. Please hear me when I say that asking for prophetic words the way the world consults fortune-tellers is a fast track to error.

(The Bible warns against dabbling with all forms of psychic readings.)

As we seek God, it's best not to focus on asking about the future. It's not about picking and choosing which pieces of information we think God should give us. Rather, we listen for what He wants to tell us, and then gratefully accept whatever that happens to be.

God may be silent about your marital future. He may ask you to simply wait in faith. He may assure you that you'll marry one day by giving you a vision of yourself in a bridal gown. But, if He does, don't presume who the groom will be if God didn't clearly reveal it.

In fairness, it's beyond difficult for a woman to receive even an in-part promise of marriage without filling in the blanks with a name (and trying out her first name with his last). As hard as we try to hold the reins, we let our hearts reflexively gallop with the possibilities.

All of this is why seeking counsel about these things can be so helpful. It can remind our often-misleading hearts to consider exactly what God said or showed us, before our hopes started to embellish with a name or fuse with a face. It can remind us to trust that God will bring exactly what He has spoken to pass, even if our human hopes disappoint.

No doubt, there are times when counsel reveals that God hasn't been speaking about a particular man, but there are also those exciting times when God uses prophetic counsel to confirm that He has, indeed, been revealing His specific intent to us.

A Funny Thing Happened On the Way to the Altar

After being single much longer than she wanted to be, my dear friend, Cheryl McKay, had been asking God about a man in her life. He was a very attentive in-town guy who was already like a best friend to her. Suddenly, after many years, an old acquaintance from her cross-country hometown began to openly pursue her. Though they didn't know each other very well, this man appeared to have an unspoken confidence that Cheryl was The One for him.

Cheryl and I made this a frequent subject of prayer. While numerous indicators had practically screamed that it was one man, a bigger prophetic picture began to emerge about the other.

You see, Cheryl is a prolific screenwriter in the entertainment industry. A few years before, she had written a screenplay called *Never the Bride* and co-authored the novel version that followed. (We're currently working on getting it made into a feature film.)

Never the Bride was written very quickly, almost as if God Himself had downloaded it for Cheryl to bring to life on the page. Though the story was fictional, God inspired Cheryl to turn her own pain over singleness into a romantic comedy, telling the tale of a woman very much like herself who had railed at God for not writing her love story, until He showed up to face her charges.

Meanwhile, in real life, Cheryl wrestled with the decision about how long to hold out for the in-town guy vs. whether or not to give the out-of-towner a chance. She kept me abreast of everything she believed she was hearing and seeing along the way. I was even with her to witness some signposts that seemed far beyond coincidental. But were those signs really from God? At the time, they seemed more puzzling than confirming.

Admittedly, even though we have both heard clearly from God on other matters, from a human standpoint, it was confusing to both of us. We were both way too close to be objective short of a clear, confirmed word from God, so we pleaded with God for an answer.

One day, the picture God was painting began to clear a bit for me. I emailed Cheryl, telling her that despite the way she'd been leaning, I didn't think that she should count the man who seemed to be a longer shot out. It was starting to dawn on me that what God might be saying was that even though *Never the Bride* had been written years before as a fictional work, it would prove to be prophetic in Cheryl's own true love story. Especially striking were the many ways one particular man mirrored the man Cheryl had unwittingly written as God's intended for the heroine of *Never the Bride*.

I tell this story to you because Cheryl's longing to hear from God about just who He wanted for her ended conclusively one Sunday, months later, when she prayerfully submitted herself for objective prophetic counsel. All of those prior misleading words and signals were readily discerned as false in light of God's true prophetic voice that day.

You'll have to read Cheryl's non-fiction companion book *Finally the Bride: Finding Hope While Waiting* for a full account of her compelling true story. For now, let's just say that all those mixed messages and confusion vanished as she was given clear, specific, divine confirmation.

Finally, Cheryl was sure she had God's answer.

Finally, she had a know-that-you-know peace.

And finally, she became a bride.

So, take heart about seeking godly judgment about what you believe God might be saying. Sometimes counsel reveals that God is giving us the desire of our hearts. It's those other times that keep us hiding in our secret corners.

The reason we avoid seeking counsel about things we believe God is saying to us is that we fear that our counselors will try to disabuse us of the notion that a particular word we've heard really is from God. If we have our hearts set too firmly on a particular result, as the Scripture says, we can fall of our own doing. We fall into the error of believing a lie. We fall into a love that will never be requited. Worse yet, we could end up in a relationship that God knows is anything but good for us.

What God Wants for His Daughters

Our heavenly Father loves His girls, far beyond the very best of human fathers. He knows it's not good for us to be alone. He doesn't want to dash our hopes. However, He does want to save us from the often heart-wrenching peril of wrongly attributing messages to Him. He wants to bring us into the safety of His truth. Even if that means we're disappointed to face the truth at first, God knows it's a truth that will set us free.

Disappointed? Maybe you think *devastated* would better describe your feelings.

Let's be honest with each other and admit that it can be painful to realize we haven't heard from God as we had hoped. Let's acknowledge the fact that He wants us to learn to distinguish His voice from the voices of any others, knowing it's for our ultimate good.

If it wasn't God's voice, then you might ask: w*ho else's?*

Simply put, when sound-minded people hear a voice that's not coming from another human being, there are only three possible sources. We're hearing:

1) the voice of God (or His messenger);
2) the voice of the enemy (or his henchman);
3) or the voice of our own hearts' desires.

Remember: God isn't a cosmic kill-joy. He's our adoring Abba Father in heaven. He understands the aching desire of our hearts to be known and loved. He also knows there is great wisdom in seeking counsel about the things we believe we're hearing from Him. He knows that when it comes to matters of our own hearts, those less intimately involved can be in a better position to discern just who may be talking to us. He wants us to let them help.

When we ask if God is saying a particular person is The One, that means that there is at least some level of uncertainty or confusion: Was it the voice of the enemy? Was it the voice of my heart's desire? Was it the voice of a man, speaking out of his interest in me? Was it just my friend's hope for me talking? Or was it, indeed, the voice of God, who knows and loves us best?

Just as the Scripture says, God doesn't want us to be confused about what He's saying to us. When He does speak, He wants us to know it's from Him. On the other hand, He wants to help clear up any misunderstanding when it's not His voice we're hearing. Sometimes, it can take a while to sort out just who said what. So, it's best not to act on what we believe we're hearing until God has clearly confirmed Himself.

If you're anything like me, you love God dearly and long to hear His voice, no matter what He has to say. Since it's such a joy to hear God's voice, I frequently remind myself that, when we're exhorted to seek prophecy, we're being encouraged to hear His voice to edify others rather than just seeking to hear from Him about our lives.

Still, there are those times when He does speak to us personally, sometimes even about the big stuff, like who He'd bless us to marry. As heavenly Father of the bride, it stands to reason that He'd have an opinion.

What's Free Will Got to Do With It?

For me, the question isn't so much *if God speaks* as it is *if God spoke a particular thing* that we believe we're hearing. If God did speak, it's important to remember exactly what it was that He said (and didn't), especially when it involves the free-will choice of another person.

It's possible that God may identify a good candidate to you. It's possible He may even give that man a nudge in your direction, offering him the opportunity to consider you. But God saying that He would *approve* of a certain match is a long way from Him categorically stating that a particular man will ultimately be The One for you.

It can be frustrating, sure enough. But lest we blame God if things don't work out, let's remember it's up to us, as free-will beings, to choose. Even if God suggests you to a man, God will not violate that man's free will to choose you or not. No attempts to name-him-and-claim-him or speak your marriage into being will bear good fruit if God didn't say it. It will only sour in your heart over time and leave you devastated. That's why it's so important to be sure about exactly what God is and isn't saying.

One thing we know for certain is that if God really did say it, it will come to pass. God does not speak idle words. They are living and active. Just as He created the universe with mere words, He speaks things into existence.

As a part of His omniscient nature, God does know which marriages will take place. He knows which ones will succeed, and He may, on occasion, encourage certain unions. I know of a number of instances where He has done just that. If and when He does speak, we know that His words have the power to accomplish and prosper, just as Isaiah prophesied:

> *"So shall my word be that goes forth from My mouth: it shall not return to Me empty, without accomplishing what I desire, and without succeeding in the matter for which I sent it."*
>
> *Isaiah 55:11*

So, if God truly told you (or someone else) that a particular man was The One for you, those weren't empty words. If God said it, you can count on it. On the other hand, you may end up sorely disappointed if you were listening to anyone else's voice.

Sadly, all too often, God, who never spoke a particular word attributed to Him, takes the brunt of our anger when what we hope for fails to materialize. It also grieves Him when we've allowed ourselves to be misguided by things He simply hasn't spoken.

Even among the faithful, I've heard more than a few comment that they are immediately wary when someone starts a sentence with: "*God told me.*" It's understandable, given how easy it can be to mistake the source of the voice we're hearing, to be misled, and to spread a misattributed quote to others, especially about things we hope are true.

When it comes to romantic pursuits, discerning just who's talking can be incredibly difficult. Often, in the quiet intimacy of our prayer lives, even in the safety of the One who knows and loves us best, our hearts' desires so easily spring to the surface and become the dominant voice. Those human desires are so deep, so strong that they sing out, a chorus of seeming direction, telling us what we so long to hear. Confirmations can seem to spring up everywhere around us, in light of what we believe we've heard. Even those who love us can be misled by their own desires for us and thus attribute the voices of their own hopes for us to God.

Did You Really Say That, God?

Many years ago, when I was single, I got into an oddball situation where God showed me the folly of misattributing the voice of a human heart's desires. Don't get the wrong impression. I'd done plenty of time as a wallflower, pining over guys who didn't return my interest.

Honestly, it's not like this kind of thing had ever happened to me before, but once, within the space of less than an hour, I heard from three believers who were seriously interested in me. It was like some kind of surreal dating show.

The phone rang. A nice guy I'd seen a few times casually—enough to know he wasn't for me—called to persuade me to give him another chance. He said that God had told him I was The One. As nicely as I could, I explained that God hadn't confirmed that to me.

Minutes later, the phone rang again. This time, it was a former boyfriend. He was calling to tell me he'd had an epiphany about us, that he wanted to get back together because—you guessed it—God had told him I was The One.

Seriously?

There are sometimes I just have to smile at God. This was one of them. I knew better than to preen over the attention. That *so* wasn't what this was about. It was crystal clear that God was teaching me a little object lesson, up close and personal. It seemed that at least one of the two guys who had called must have misattributed the voice of his own heart's desires—maybe even both.

What I didn't know was that God's lesson wasn't over. Incredibly, the phone rang again. This time it was Bachelor Number Three, a guy who had expressed an interest in me weeks before. After One and Two's calls, with both claiming divine proclamation that we were God's choices for each other, you can imagine how I felt. My head was reeling when I picked up the phone and heard Three on the line.

When I confided in Three about what had just happened, he said something I truly appreciated. He told me that he could see I needed time and that he didn't want me to feel any pressure from him. He was content to step aside and give me the time I needed to pray and allow God to speak to me. He was man enough to let his interest in me stand unanswered, and he made no attempt to sway my choice by claiming an endorsement from God.

Impressed, I spent some time getting to know Three. To tell you the truth, I ping-ponged between attraction and abject terror during the first six months. I was afraid that he would push me into a committed relationship faster than I was ready to go, but he never did. Two and a half years later, I married him. Eventually, he told me that he had known I was The One he'd marry, before that surreal string of calls. That quiet faith had kept him at rest while he waited for my heart to catch up with his, till we stood at the altar—God, he and I—uniting as that three-fold cord that is not easily broken. Indeed, as of this writing, we have been married more than three decades.

My take-away from this may surprise you. Setting the issue of who heard God's voice or didn't aside, in the end I believe all three of these guys did the right thing. It's something I'll encourage you to do whenever you're convinced God is saying a particular person is The One for you: have the maturity to declare your interest.

At a loss for how to do that? There's help in the next chapter.

THREE

Defining the Relationship

"Better is open rebuke than love that is concealed."

Proverbs 27:5

Yikes, right? I know it's hard, and I completely understand if even the thought of what I'm about to propose freaks you out a little (or a lot!). But since the Bible says it's better to confess love than to conceal it, we need to woman up about it.

Defining The Relationship (a.k.a. D.T.R.) is *so* not something a woman wants to be forced to initiate. If it's any consolation, just about everyone cowers at the idea of broaching the dreaded D.T.R. subject.

School kids coax their friends to check for receptivity first. Remember that? You may have even sent or received one of those *"Do you like me?"* notes with little boxes to check *yes*, *no*, or *maybe*.

I sent one of those notes. It was a dodge, so I could avoid actually having to look my sixth grade classmate in the eyes to get an answer. Admittedly, that was kind of cute at age twelve, but hopefully as we mature we can find the courage to face our fears, gaze into that man's eyes, and have a grown-up D.T.R. conversation.

Remember Rachel? She's the woman who kept hearing that *"Not now"* and asked me if God was saying that Keith was The One for her. Among the first questions I asked her was this:

Does he know how you feel?

Rachel's response pleased me. She had already braved a D.T.R. with Keith. She was in the process of waiting to see if their best friendship could grow into something more.

Maybe you've been throwing hints out there. Some of you have been pelting your guy with hints for ages, hoping he'll get the idea that you're interested, but all your hints fly right over his seemingly clueless head.

If a man is actively considering you, he may pick up on your subtle suggestions. But he may not. I've seen perfectly intelligent men need a woman to spell out her interest before they really get down to the business of considering her, especially if that man is already in a satisfying platonic friendship with that woman.

It doesn't mean you're walking into a rejection that a man doesn't get what you're trying to say indirectly. In fact, I know a number of women who've braved the dreaded D.T.R. and gotten a welcomed "yes" in return.

One of them was my mother.

The Teddy Turtletoe Factor

After seeing each other for some time in church youth group circles, my mom and dad went to colleges in different states. While they continued to communicate by mail, no commitment whatsoever had been voiced.

After a while, my mom's good looks caught the attention of another guy at her school. This isn't his real name, but we'll call him Teddy Turtletoe. (With all respect to any real Turtletoes out there, Teddy's actual name was smile-inducing, very much along those lines.)

Back to our story: Teddy Turtletoe made no secret of his interest in pursuing my mother. She knew she was more interested in my dad, but since he wasn't giving her so much as an inkling if they had any kind of future together, she braved a straightforward D.T.R. letter.

Mom declared herself by writing that she was far more interested in seeing where things could go with my dad if he felt the same way. If, however, my dad didn't see the possibilities of a future with her, she would accept that, move on, and give Teddy Turtletoe a chance.

This was long before the instant gratification of email or social networking. Snail mail took even longer back then, but within a matter of days, Mom's wait to know how my dad felt about her was over. She told me that as soon as my dad got that letter, he jumped on the next bus north to her college. He promptly "pinned" my mom, as was traditional in those days, and then married her the next summer.

Playing the Teddy Turtletoe card doesn't always work out the way it did for my mom and dad, but it can still be for the best if you're in a desired-but-undefined relationship when another man comes calling. It didn't take two seconds for my dad to realize he wanted a life with my mom once he was faced with the possibility of losing her. On the other hand, if a woman plunks down the Teddy Turtletoe card and the guy she's more interested in doesn't respond, that's a very broad hint from him that it's time to fold and explore other possibilities.

Hearing His Hints

Just as women do, men throw out their share of hints. You're wise to factor in any hints before investing your heart too deeply in someone who is trying to tell you he just wants to be friends. As hard as it may be to accept it, if he's attempting to set you up with someone else or if he mentions noticing another woman, he may be hinting that he's not interested in you romantically himself.

If he refers to you simply as a friend, he may be saying that's how he prefers to relate to you. If he makes a point of saying that he likes to be the pursuer, yet he keeps things platonic with you, that may be his way of breaking it to you gently that he's not interested in pursuing you.

If you're willing to accept his hints as his answer and let go without a direct rejection, then you can avoid the D.T.R. talk and move on with your life. Know yourself. If hope in the possibility keeps you hanging, if you're really still wondering what he thinks or if he's even considered you, there's nothing like a D.T.R. confab to break a friendship out of a going-nowhere cycle. He may say *"Yes."* He may say *"No."* He may need to think and pray about it for the first time. But as the Bible tells us, it's better to endure an open rebuke than to suffer through the heartache of unconfessed love.

Women as Initiators

Some women hesitate to be the first to suggest that a man consider a relationship, feeling that it's a violation of spiritual protocol. They wait, hoping that the man will speak up first, even when they're convinced that God has given His Fatherly stamp of approval. But did you know the Bible supports women as D.T.R. initiators?

Check out the story of a widowed Moabitess in the book of Ruth. Notice how specifically Naomi laid out a plan for Ruth to declare her interest to Boaz, in keeping with the customs of their day:

> *"Wash yourself therefore, and anoint yourself, and put on your best clothes, and go down to the threshing floor, but do not make yourself known to the man, until he has finished eating and drinking. And it shall be, when he lies down, that you shall*

> *notice the place where he lies, and you shall
> go and uncover his feet and lie down; then
> he will tell you what you shall do."*
>
> Ruth 3:3–4

Today's customs don't include this particular mode of declaration. Still, the basics of this act, blessed by God and recorded in Scripture, have application today.

Keep in mind: this was no subtle hint that Ruth was instructed to throw. There was nothing veiled about her intent. Lying at a man's feet in that day was as direct as a no-holds-barred D.T.R. is today. So, if it's time for a D.T.R. with someone in your life, then you might want to apply the following modern-day version of Naomi's advice:

Bathe Yourself

Naturally, you'll want to look freshly scrubbed. You'll want to have a clean aroma about you. It wouldn't hurt to be having a good hair day.

Did you know that Esther went through an entire year of purification? She was anointed with myrrh for six months, and then another six months with sweet perfumes, all before she presented herself to the King for consideration.

Now, I'm not suggesting that a year of beautification is in order before you can have your D.T.R. It's just that cleansing and grooming will help prepare you to look and feel your best for the occasion. Pluck those stray eyebrows and trim your nails, if needed. Simple is best. This isn't a time to make yourself over into what you are not. This is a time you'll want to feel like the best, freshly groomed version of who you are.

As you tend to the exteriors, invite the Lord to also cleanse you internally. If there are things that need tidying up in your heart, ask God to help you with that purifying process. Remember when Jesus asked to wash Peter's feet and Peter refused Him at first? It's true that allowing the Lord to cleanse and groom our spirits is an incredibly intimate act. It's a time when we drop our fig leaves and come out of hiding, trusting that the Lord who made us understands our reluctance. He wants us to come naked and unashamed into His presence. And just as He, the Lord of all, knelt to wash the grime of the day off Peter's feet, He waits to cleanse you.

Put on Fresh Clothing

Naomi told Ruth to put on her best clothes. Though your best clothes may be formal wear, obviously you won't want to go that far unless you'll be having this conversation at a black tie event. Clearly, Naomi's point was that she wanted Ruth to dress in something other than what Boaz had seen her gleaning in day-to-day. As you weigh your clothing options, you may be asking yourself: how nice is too nice?

Choose something that's modestly attractive, something you're comfortable wearing. You may feel tempted to over do it. But bear in mind that—as far as he's concerned—this is not a date. Don't put extra pressure on yourself by taking a fashion risk. It's fine if you want to wear something he hasn't seen before, something that's flattering on you. You just won't want to feel overdressed.

This isn't a matter of selling him based on the externals. It's first and foremost about letting him see the inner beauty of your heart. Don't stress over the clothes. They won't make or break it. Just wear something you'll feel good about having on regardless of his response.

Take special time out for the Lord before you go to meet him. Inwardly, did you know God wants to go beyond bathing you to clothing your spirit? As surely as God spoke through Zechariah that He wanted to take away Joshua's filthy garments and clothe him with rich apparel, He waits to do that for you (Zechariah 3:4). The Bible says that He will clothe you as with jewels, just as a bride is adorned (Isaiah 49:18). This isn't about a physical wedding gown or accessories. It's about so much more. It's about allowing God to clothe you with a gentle and quiet spirit, with the adornments of grace and dignity (Proverbs 31:25).

To some, this may seem a long way to go to have a simple D.T.R. chat. Truth is: you can follow Naomi's counsel to the letter, but it still won't guarantee your guy's response. But if you carefully attend to Naomi's instructions to Ruth, if you allow God to clothe you with the power of His Spirit, you will go into what could otherwise be a nerve-racking talk full of the fruit of His peace, no matter the outcome.

Choose Your Moment Wisely

Notice how specifically Naomi counseled Ruth about finding the right moment to declare herself to Boaz. Consider what the appropriate time might be for you. It should be an hour when you know he'll be relaxed, not pressured by the cares of the day. For your sake as well as his, avoid mealtime. If he's a sports nut, make sure you won't have to compete with the television for his attention. Wait until he's off work, has been well fed, when he can sit with you and focus on what you have to say.

Consult your heavenly Father about the timing. He will help you with this if you'll take a moment to request it. While you're at it, you can ask the Lord to go before you, to prepare this man's heart for what you're going to say. You can always just wait for the right moment to strike as many do, but you may not feel as confident about it as you would if you sit with the Lord and allow Him to lead you about when this important conversation should take place.

Find a Good Spot to Talk

Naomi was very specific about where Ruth should make her move and you are well advised to think about that, too. It's not that you need to find a threshing floor as Ruth did. It's not a formula to be followed in a literal sense. But there is great merit in considering what the right setting might be.

For your sake and his, keep this conversation between the two of you. If others are within earshot, it may make it harder for both of you to feel at ease while having this talk. So, it may be best if you choose a place that is reasonably private.

There's no need to make a big production of it, in fact, the simpler the better. You could plan to talk to him at your place or his, or outside on a park bench if the weather is nice. Just keep in mind that you'll want to be situated where you can part shortly after you've said what you have to say. He'll probably need to have time to process things alone, so plan to give him that space.

Be Clear and Concise

In Ruth's day, lying at a man's feet as she was told to do sent a clear message. It was an extremely bold move. (Had it not been for Naomi's trust in Boaz's godly character, it could have also been considered perilous.)

Today, when a man gets on one knee at a woman's feet and opens a ring box, we know what it means. These are quick signals that speak a thousand words. Naomi knew that Boaz would immediately understand Ruth's act as a declaration of her marital interest in him.

Perhaps it goes without saying that lying at a man's feet would be considered very invasive and a highly inappropriate mode of declaration in today's culture. Still, the point remains that, like Ruth, you should prepare yourself to communicate exactly what you mean in a concise manner. Many women are far more verbose than men. This is one of those times when less will be more. For your sake and his, plan to make this a relatively short conversation. Resist the urge to dodge, ramble, hint, or to be anything less than clear about your interest in him.

Overwhelmed about how to put this into words? It could be just this simple:

> *"I want to let you in on something I've been praying about. So far, we've just been friends, but I'm wondering whether you and I have the potential to go beyond that into more of an intentional dating relationship. I know that's something I'd be interested in exploring with you. No need to answer now...I just wanted to put it out there and give you some time to consider it, too. Would you pray about this and let me know?"*

Do you see how these five sentences (or your version of them) are all you'd need? Let's break it down:

1. The first sentence lets him know this is something you think is important enough to pray about. Hopefully, that will get his attention.

2. That second sentence gets right to the point, something most men appreciate.

3. Your third sentence underscores your interest in him. You might think it's implicit, but trust me. Step out on that limb and say it. Men fear rejection as much as women do. They want to know that if they ask you out, you're almost certain to say *"Yes."*

4. Sentence four reassures him that you don't expect an immediate response, and that you're going to give him some private time with this.

5. Finally, the question this all boils down to wraps it up, only asking something he can easily agree to do, which is to seek God about you for himself.

Still with me?

You may look at this and think I don't get your situation. Maybe this guy isn't the praying type. But if he's not and you are, how much common ground do you have with him on a spiritual level anyway? God doesn't make a practice of leading His daughters into unequally yoked relationships. He knows you need a man who not only shares your faith, but who is willing to at least pray about this.

Maybe he is a man of God, perhaps even a man of prayer. That may be part of the attraction you feel. However, even if you truly believe God is saying this man is The One for you, it's usually best to resist claiming God's endorsement. Just as God respects your free will to choose who is of serious interest to you, allow this man that same privilege. Exert no pressure. Honestly admit your own interest and give him the freedom to choose.

Allow a Season of Time

Go back and look over Naomi's last bit of instruction to Ruth. She buttoned her counsel with words to remember: *"...and he will tell you what you shall do."*

Once you've braved your part of the D.T.R., it's time to wait. If he's already prayed about it, he may answer you on the spot, but don't count on it. Be prepared to exit his company gracefully at that point. Allow him to take it from there and get back to you. Don't request or expect an immediate response, no matter how crazy it drives you to wait.

As much as you may want to stick around to see how he reacts, understand that carpooling with him anywhere after a D.T.R. can get more than awkward. For that reason, it's often a good idea to drive in separate vehicles or walk. Remember, you've had plenty of time to think and pray about this before the D.T.R. He may want you to stay and talk about it more, but be fully prepared to give him the gift of alone-time to consider things afterward. Just ask him to get back to you within a few days with his answer: either *yes*, *no*, or *I'm not sure yet*.

Walk away, knowing that this is a victory, any way it goes. After you've left him, use the time apart to continue to seek God yourself.

If he doesn't get back to you within a week, send a breezy request for his answer. If he doesn't reply, assume it's a *no* and he just doesn't have the heart to say it. If he gives you a *yes*, then follow Naomi's advice and let him tell you where he sees things going from there. If he answers that he's *not sure yet*, let him know you are willing to give him more time, if he intends to make it a matter of purposed prayer.

If he does ask for time to pray about the possibilities, give him a season to seek the Lord. When I say a season, I mean literally a season: three months at the very most. He may answer you much sooner, but if he doesn't, once that three-month season has elapsed without a response, it's time to graciously accept what is known as a "slow no" and walk away. It's time to allow God to heal and redirect your heart.

Though most who will reply do so sooner than later, I have seen a number of men take such a season of prayer very seriously and come back after weeks, even as much as two to three months and still have a positive answer. I have seen marriages result. However, in my experience with female-initiated declarations, I've never known a guy to come back with romantic interest in a woman he's always considered a platonic friend if it's been more than three months. I've known former couples to reunite after longer periods apart, but if a guy has never seen a gal-pal *that way* and doesn't come back with interest within three months, it's time to accept his unspoken *no*.

It's sad to say, but I've seen numerous women wait for years after a D.T.R., hanging onto hope, even turning away the interest of other believing men out of a misplaced sense of faithfulness.

Woman of God, your heavenly Father wants better for you.

Allow God to lead you to still waters, to cleanse you afresh, and do a new work in your heart. Take comfort in the knowledge that you did the right thing. You were honest and mature enough to declare yourself, and you are respectful enough of his free will choice to let him go.

If, on the other hand, the guy responds to your D.T.R. with a level of interest within that season, try not to rush ahead of him. Remember, you just asked him if he'd be willing to explore an intentional dating relationship. So, if he says he is, it's just that—an exploration—not a proposal of marriage. Intentional dating is about testing the potential of long-range marital compatibility, for sure. But keep in mind that he may have a lot if catching up to do with you in the feelings and commitment departments.

One final thought about the dreaded D.T.R: don't dread it. It's a high-wire cross, a thrill ride—no doubt about it. But rather than dreading the fact that you're faced with initiating this D.T.R., thank God for it.

Thank God that He loves you and knows what's best for you. Thank God that He's got your back. Thank God the truth that will come out of defining this relationship will set you free, one way or another.

Have confidence. If he is truly the man God says is The One for you, it will come to pass. If he isn't, the sooner you find that out, the better. Enjoy the adventure in faith that life is and let the current of God's grace take you wherever He wills.

FOUR

Things God Definitely Said

> *"For the word of God is living and active, and sharper than any two-edged sword, and piercing as far as the division of soul and spirit, of both joints and marrow, and able to discern the thoughts and intentions of the heart."*
>
> *Hebrews 4:12*

In the midst of confusion, mixed signals, and downright deception, one thing is for certain: God is definitely speaking to us through the truth of His Word.

No matter who believes they hear what, if it's in conflict with Scripture, it should be immediately rejected as false. That established, lest we think the Bible doesn't speak to romantic relationships, we have only to peruse the book nestled in the center of it: the shamelessly passionate Song of Solomon.

Though the Bible was written thousands of years ago, it is still and will always remain just as the book of Hebrews states it to be: living, active, and sharp. It cuts deep into the core of our beings. It helps us to discern the difference between the often-misleading motivations of our souls and the always dependable voice of the indwelling Holy Spirit.

What does the soul vs. the spirit have to do with romance? In a word: everything.

The soul is the center of the will, the heart, the mind. It's that uniquely human part of you that God sets free to choose. Figuratively, the soul is the heart, in that it wants what it wants. The heart desires. Have you ever noticed that your heart has a voracious appetite? It can literally eat you out of house and home. The worldly may encourage us to follow our hearts, but check out what the Bible says about this soulish organ:

> *"The heart is more deceitful than all else, and is desperately sick: who can understand it?"*
>
> *Jeremiah 17:9*

Deceitful? Desperately sick? *Really?*
Really.

We assume that we know our own hearts, but the Bible suggests it's much harder than we think. Love songs may compel us to chase our hearts' desires. But Scripture cautions that our hearts—those ravenously wanting souls of ours—are infamous for leading us into terrible choices.

Our hearts are a muscle-bound, impressionable bag of tricks. Our souls are what desperately need saving. That's why it's so important that we let the Word of God pierce the deepest part of who we are and differentiate our fallible hearts from our sanctified spirits.

Our spirits need to be filled continually with the Holy Spirit of God, who promises to teach us and guide us, especially as we're faced with important life choices, like who a good husband might be (John 14:26). That's even more the case when we believe God is speaking to us specifically about that choice Himself.

Indeed, there are times when God may speak to someone about considering a potential spouse. He has definitely been known to harden or soften a heart. But what God will never do is force anyone's hand. We are made in His image and one of the characteristics of God is that He has the ability to choose. He chose to create us with that same ability, and He doesn't violate our free will to exercise our own choices, even the choice of whether or not to obey Him.

Consider Hosea. Though he obeyed God, Hosea had the option to turn down the Almighty's directive to take a harlot as his wife. He also had the option when it came to which specific woman among many he would choose when he personally opted for Gomer.

Think of Rebekah. Even after Rebekah fulfilled the signs Abraham's servant sought in selecting a wife for Isaac, Rebekah and her family still had the free-will choice of whether to or not to agree to the union.

Isaac could have rejected Rebekah, but didn't.

Yes. There is clear biblical precedent for God setting up a relationship ala Adam and Eve. (*But really, who else didn't have a choice?*) However, the far more common post-Eden directive of Scripture is that God doesn't make puppets of us. Instead, He gives us broad, acceptable parameters within which to choose.

Just as God commanded it should be for Zelophehad's daughters in Numbers 36:6, we are free to marry the person we please, as long as it's someone within the family of our faith.

Finding First Love

Ah, the joys of a first love! It's quite an experience to feel something in your heart for someone, a love unlike what you've ever felt for anyone else. It's as if that special someone is the sun and your whole life orbits around him. You look at that face and everything in you shines—or melts! He becomes the subject of every love song you hear.

Think about that person your soul loves more than any other. It's okay. Go ahead. Call his name aloud to the heavens in prayer.

Now tell me. Honestly.

Is it God?

Okay, don't feel badly if you were only thinking in terms of a human love. If you were, you can read back through the first two paragraphs of this section as an exercise, with God in mind this time. As you do, monitor yourself. Does the thought of God as a first love make your heart sing? Do you adore Him above and beyond all human loves?

There's not necessarily anything wrong with loving that man in your life. There could be everything right about it. When we truly love human beings, it pleases God. We fulfill the second of two commandments Jesus cited as the greatest (Mark 12:30–31). It's just important to always keep that first commandment—to love God—first.

Did you know that even a believer could become an idol in your heart before God? It doesn't happen all at once, but day-by-day, we can let that man become more important to us than God. We can allow our desires for a godly husband to eclipse our desire for the Lover of our souls. So, even if that man in your life shares your faith, it's a good idea to regularly examine your heart in light of this verse from God's Word:

> *"But I have this against you, that you have left your first love."*
>
> *Revelation 2:4*

When my niece, Bethany, checked her heart along these lines, she couldn't help thinking about her friend, Drew. Drew loved God with a passion, just the way Bethany did. They had developed a strong friendship and had much in common. Both had signed up for a summer mission trip to Africa through their church, to serve the needy there. All seemed well. But was it?

A month or two before the trip, Bethany contacted me. She said that as she had begun to prepare her heart to go to Africa, she'd had a troubling sense that something was out of balance. Bethany told me that her feelings for Drew went beyond the platonic friendship they enjoyed. It wasn't so much that Drew didn't seem to share her feelings that bothered her. She had weathered other romantic disappointments and was resolved to get through this one. No, the problem went much deeper.

Bethany confessed that as much as she had been looking forward to serving God in Africa, it was the idea of going there with Drew that stirred her heart the most. Drew had become too important to her, and she realized she had to do something about it. She wanted to put her desire for Drew into the right perspective. She needed to recalibrate her heart and reaffirm God as her first love.

I've always adored Bethany. I've long respected her pure relationship with God. My love and admiration for her only grew when she told me what she had done. Bethany explained to Drew that she'd developed feelings for him, beyond what he apparently felt for her. She told Drew straight out that she realized she needed step back from him and reorder her heart. She knew that she needed to go on the mission trip out of pure love for God. It wouldn't be right for her motivation to come from anything or anyone else.

Bethany told Drew that she'd decided to fast from personal contact with him over the remaining weeks before the trip. She needed to refocus on God as her first love. It was a one-way D.T.R., with no expectation of a response. The only reason Bethany told Drew was so he would understand what was going on when she curtailed personal contact.

God saw Bethany's heart. He knew He had been restored to first place as soon as Bethany took the step of faith to have this talk with Drew. He also had a surprise waiting for my dear niece.

Though Bethany went into this conversation with Drew assuming that would be the end with him, it wasn't. Instead, Drew responded with openness. He said he'd like to take some time pray about the possibilities.

So, Drew joined Bethany in fasting from personal contact with her during the month before the mission trip. They ended the fast by serving side-by-side in Africa, with God as their first love. After Bethany and Drew returned, they felt God's blessing about beginning to date. Imagine our joy in the spring of 2011, when we gathered as a family to witness their wedding vows, as their hearts were united in Christ.

It doesn't always turn out this way when a woman restores God to His rightful place in her heart. But we know that it always turns out for that woman's best.

> *"And we know that God causes all things to work together for good to those who love God, to those who are called according to His purpose."*
>
> *Romans 8:28*

Sisters, hang onto that promise.

Trust that your love life is among the "all things" God is working out for your good. Walk along His continuum of grace, your hand clasping your Savior's. Do not look back; do not look to the right or the left. Know that making Him first in your heart keeps you square on the path to true love.

In time, you may notice that a man is walking alongside you, following Jesus, just as you are. You won't have to manipulate things. When it's right, he'll be as interested in you as you are in him. It will be effortless to choose each other and to enjoy the blessing of the God who loved you first.

Missionary Relationships

Did you wince a little when you read this heading?

I guess it's to be expected that in broaching this sensitive topic, I might inadvertently step on a few toes. Please accept my apologies if I do cause a pang or two in the course of reading this book. Solomon called the wounds of a friend "faithful" as I hope any wounds I cause are. But I realize wounds still hurt, no matter how skillful the surgeon. I'm no physician. To tell the truth, I get woozy at the sight of blood—kind of the way you may feel as you consider the things I'm about to say. Please think of me as a friend, one who cares deeply about women, one who understands how difficult it can be to truly follow God when men sweep us off our feet.

So, here we go.

While the directive to marry only within the faith is clear in Scripture, some are quick to point out that the Bible isn't specific about dating. Add the plummeting marriage rate and the reluctance of a growing number of believing men to even ask a woman out and you can see why so many of God's daughters resort to exploring secular options.

It doesn't feel like blatantly defying God to jump through what seems like a Scriptural loophole. We justify dating outside the fold further by explaining that we hope to be a good witness to the unbeliever. We assure our confidants that we'd never go so far as to marry outside our faith. We blame believing men for living for themselves and dodging commitment. We defend our choices by observing how much more "Christian" the unbeliever seems than the actual believing men in our circles. We rationalize that it's only a date.

But is it?

Transparency time, Sisters. For any woman who hopes to marry, it is never just a date. Let's be honest. Even with non-believers, from the moment attraction strikes, we reflexively start to consider a man's potential in our lives. The more attracted we are, the more our hearts begin to automatically wrap themselves around the possibility that he might be The One.

The newness of a growing relationship coupled with the rush of attraction leads us farther down the road. Incrementally, we begin to extend our boundaries, and before we realize what's hit us, we've fallen fall in love. We pray fervently for this man's salvation, frantic to retrofit him as acceptable husband material, desperate to have the blessing of our heavenly Father.

I've seen it go this way with multiple believers who have pursued unequally yoked relationships. Their stories are essentially the same. I'd share them with you, but even with changed names I'm reluctant to expose these women to any more shame and heartbreak than they have already endured. I've seen God extend special grace to those women who came to faith after marrying as non-believers, but I've never seen it work out well when a believer knowingly marries outside the faith.

Granted, though the Bible is overt in stating that believers are only to marry other believers, some are quick to point out that there's no verse in the Bible that literally prohibits dating a non-believer. Dating wasn't even a word that was used back in the day, so there are no literal references to *dating*, at least not by that term. However, there are numerous applicable exhortations about maintaining sexual purity, the kind of company we keep, and being in the world but not of the world. There are cautions about not letting anyone draw us away from our commitment to God. Fact is, the Bible offers plenty of pertinent wisdom for singles who have ears to hear.

Scripture has a lot to say about building a house—about where God wants us to build, about the importance of a firm foundation, and about how we are cautioned to consider the cost before we embark upon building a tower (Luke 14:28-30). Take a look at these words of Jesus that Matthew recorded:

> *"And everyone who hears these words of Mine, and does not act upon them, will be like a foolish man who built his house upon*

the sand. And the rain descended, and the floods came, and the winds blew, and burst against that house; and it fell, and great was its fall."

Matthew 7:26–27

In the figurative language of Scripture, a house can be understood to mean much more than just a physical dwelling. Our bodies are said to be the dwelling place of the Holy Spirit from the moment we commit to relationship with Christ and ask Him to take up residence in us (I Corinthians 6:19).

It's really no stretch to apply these structure-building passages to the relationships we construct in our lives. It also behooves us to recognize the strong tower that God's Word can be in the dangerous world of dating. Out of love, God beckons the righteous to run into His strong tower. His Word isn't meant to deny us anything or anyone who is good for us. It is meant to protect us from the onslaughts of the enemy that we invite when we fail to build on a firm foundation of faith. God wants to save us from the catastrophic losses we stand to incur when those unstable houses come tumbling down (Psalm 61:3, Proverbs 18:10).

Take a moment to look up and really apply these passages to the process of building your life with another person. Dating a non-believer is like putting earnest money down to build a house on the shifting sands of a beach. It may look sunny when you break ground, but hurricane season is on the way. You might say it's just for fun, that you'll hold the line. But before you know it, you're investing more and more, and soon a home is being constructed in your heart.

You can't help it. You play house, instinctively. Just like a sparrow is hard-wired to build her nest, your soulful heart will automatically begin to gather twigs when you spend time with a man you find to be attractive. Every date, every call or text, every expression of affection adds to the growing framework. It quickly develops into far more than a passing fancy. Physical boundaries get crossed. Soon, it becomes a looming structure in your life. It feels welcoming. It can even look great from the outside. But it lacks an essential element your heavenly Father advises for very good reason: a spiritual foundation.

Though there is no foundation of faith to secure what you're erecting against the storms of life ahead, this unsteady structure takes shape with unexpected speed. Daydreams turn into reality. What started as a casual date becomes a regular thing. Over time, commitment to this man sneaks up on you. You announce your relationship on the internet. You introduce him as your boyfriend to your friends and family. You invest more and more of yourself into the hope that you've finally found someone to make a home with, someone to raise a family with, someone to call your own.

Dating may not equate to signing the deed on a home, but it is definitely the process by which we build one. That's why a date is never "just a date." It's better to think of it as a building project, because that's exactly what it is.

Consider what Solomon said on this subject:

> *"Unless the Lord builds the house, they labor in vain who build it; unless the Lord guards the city, the watchman keeps awake in vain."*
>
> *Psalm 127:1*

God is saying through His Word that He wants to not only be part of anything we build, He wants to build it for us. Otherwise, it doesn't matter how diligently anyone tries to keep watch: that habitation is in peril.

Indeed, there are those who erect elaborate structures without God, those who construct complex secular relationships, but believers who do so are working in vain. The Hebrew word for *vain* in this verse is used in the same sense as the word *desolating*. Literally, it means *ruin*. Figuratively, it speaks of uselessness, lying, and even idolatry.

Ouch.

Admittedly, classifying dating a non-believer as tantamount to idolatry might seem extreme to some. It may, until we realize that there are more ways to bow down to an idol than dancing around a golden calf of our own design. Idolatry is about making anything more important to us than submitting to God's Lordship—even that guy we hope is The One. Idolatry is about saying *"no"* to God and *"yes"* to the enemy, plain and simple. God makes no bones about wanting to be first in our hearts. Above all, He wants to be our greatest desire.

There are those who might be quick to cite Hosea as example of God condoning a missionary relationship, but the overriding message of God's recorded Word is that God wants us to choose between those with whom we'd be equally yoked:

> *"Do not be bound together with unbelievers; for what partnership have righteousness and lawlessness, or what fellowship has light with darkness?"*
>
> *II Corinthians 6:14*

Even within the faith, we are wise to consider how spiritually compatible we might be with another believer. The balanced voice of Scripture is that Hosea was an exception, a prophet sent into a relationship doomed to betrayal, to stand forever as a life-picture of how God's people chronically wander from His best for them.

More times than I can count, I've heard believing women defend the choice of a non-believer, stating their intent to lead the man to the Lord. Some are even convinced that God has told them a non-believer is The One. Given Hosea's experience, I won't go as far as to say that it could never happen. I'll just say it's highly unlikely that these women have heard God's voice and infinitely more likely that they are listening to the voice of their own overwhelming hearts' desires.

Sadly, many of those unequally yokes marriages I've known of have either resulted in the believer straying from the fold, or they have ended in great suffering, strife, betrayal, and often divorce. On a spiritual level they leave the believer stranded. She is left alone at church, alone in ministry, completely companionless when it comes to sharing in the most meaningful aspect of her life: relationship with God.

So, let's preserve Hosea's experience in its singular context, rather than leaping through it as biblical loophole. Moreover, let's keep in mind that when God asks us to marry within the faith, it's with our very best at heart.

Just like Adam and Eve had the choice to eat from any number of trees in the garden of Eden, except the one specific tree from which God warned them not to eat, your heavenly Father is saying that He welcomes you to choose any man within the garden of faith as The One in your life. You may be tempted to partake of that one tree God asks you not to touch. When that happens, know that any voice that tells you that a non-believer is The One for you is virtually always either the voice of your heart's desires or the voice of the enemy, and not the voice of God.

Choosing a Believer

My father used to talk about the importance of turning variables into constants in decision-making. Too many options can be confusing, so it helps to start putting certain things aside, and then setting other things into place, as a foundation upon which to build.

If you're trying to fill out the sky portion of a landscape jigsaw puzzle, it can really help to start by separating the light blue pieces from those that are clearly in earth colors. Eliminating non-believers from the dating equation can really help you in this way. It's one of those things you can know from the Bible that God is definitely saying. It's a bit of relationship guidance that's repeated in Scripture. There are also cautionary stories of those who ignored God's Fatherly advice, those who followed their hearts and paid dearly for it. Two names: Samson and Delilah.

Enough said?

Choosing a believer is always a good starting point, but don't forget—there's still that free will hurdle out there. You may have asked God about a certain available man. He may even be a spiritual leader. You may feel that God would bless the relationship and perhaps He would. (Can you hear a *but* coming?) But...even if God has spoken to you, that you two could potentially be good for each other—even if God has said the same thing to the man—that man still has free will. That means he has the option to enjoy God's blessing with any other believing woman he chooses, that is, if she also chooses him.

As much as we can tend to treat Him otherwise, the Holy Spirit does not operate like a love potion. No matter how much you plead, beg, bargain, or cajole, God will not force a man to choose you.

There's a very good reason for that. God knows you will be better off with a man who chooses you of his own accord. Just as God longs to be desired and pursued for Himself, He understands that you need more than a half-hearted man who has been talked into choosing you or pushed in your direction.

God may suggest to a man that he'd do well to consider you, but ultimately He knows that you need a man who loves you and who has the singular strength of purpose to pursue you of his own free-will choice.

Not So Eligible Men

Perhaps it would seem to go without saying that people who are already married are not among those God invites believers to choose. Nonetheless, I include this section for those of you who find yourselves in this situation.

As hard as it may be to face, if you think you hear a voice telling you that an otherwise married man is your husband, then no matter how much you want to believe it's God speaking, know that it's not.

Whether it comes to your waking ears or in a dream, a message that encourages you out of your present marriage or into the arms of a married man isn't coming from heaven. It could be the voice of the enemy, or there's an excellent chance that it's the voice of your own heart's desires.

Our hearts are renowned for misleading us in that way. Subconscious longings surface during the natural state of dreaming. As tempting as it may seem to entertain this voice or the pleasures of that dream, dear Sister—it's not for your good and it's definitely not from God.

The Bible is very clear on this subject:

God hates divorce as well as the breaking of vows that it brings about. Marriage is a covenant relationship and God is an eternal covenant keeper. He is the essence of faithfulness, so He doesn't encourage His children to be unfaithful in any way, shape, or form. To the contrary, God exhorts us to forgive and love unfailingly, the way He forgives and loves us.

In some instances—such as when a man effectively deserts his wife by making it impossible for her to safely live with him because of perilous criminal activity or domestic violence—separation or divorce may seem unavoidable. The Bible says that believers who are deserted are set free, that they are released from the bondage of marital vows broken by an unbeliever (I Corinthians 7:15). God just doesn't want us to be party to initiating the breaking of vows ourselves.

Marriage is a physical, emotional, and spiritual union that God is emphatic about preserving. Granted, there is also an exception listed in Matthew 5:32, in cases of adultery. Still, even when Gomer deserted Hosea and was unfaithful to him, and despite Israel's repeated unfaithfulness, God set the example by encouraging reconciliation. Hosea Chapter 11 tells us that God pursued His people, that He took them into His forgiving arms—even though they didn't realize that it was He who had healed them. It says that God drew them with bonds of love, that He lifted the burden from their shoulders and laid food before them.

What lengths our heavenly Father goes to show His love for us, even to those of us who wander and betray Him! God says that His heart is turned within, that His compassions are kindled. As the very tender original language of Hosea 11 expresses, the Lord is deeply affected by anything that injures and separates us from what He knows is best for us.

For those who have already suffered through the agony of divorce, please know that nothing in this is meant to heap guilt on you. As much as we should do everything possible to avoid it, the Bible does not call divorce unforgivable. There truly is no condemnation in Christ. There is mercy and grace for those who sincerely request it of the Lord.

Through the prophet Hosea, God promises:

> *"I will heal their apostasy, I will love them freely; for My anger has turned away from them."*
>
> *Hosea 14:4*

God, who has called us to peace, understands the heartbreak of divorce. He longs to save His people from that pain and suffering. He knows that those who have once broken marriage vows are more likely to break them again, a grief He longs to spare us. Still, in all our failures, He is there for us. He is there to comfort us and to bind up our broken hearts, to heal us, and draw us close into His bonds of love.

You can confirm for certain that God is saying the following things to you from His Word and proactively apply them to your situation:

Be faithful. Keep your vows. Honor the commitment any man you know has made. Do not become a sounding board for a man whose marriage is in trouble. Like Joseph ran from Potiphar's wife, put on your track shoes and sprint away from anyone who would be betraying a marriage vow to pursue you. Run into the arms of a faithful God who wants so much better for you.

Intimacies

Are you ready for me to sound crazy out-of-touch with modern mores? (*Oh, well. I'll say this anyway, because it's very in-touch with what God says through His Word to all believers.*)

Save marital intimacies for marriage, even in the privacy of your thought life.

This may seem absurd in light of common practice, even among other believers, but trust me: you will never regret obeying God in waiting for the physical intimacies God intends to be shared between a husband and wife. Wait to become one flesh until you are married.

Remember that, in exhorting us to wait, God doesn't deprive us of any good thing (Psalm 84:11). Rather, He wants to protect us from the consequences of sexual impurity. God wants your relationship to be built on a firm spiritual foundation, not on the shifting sands of physical passion.

If you're hoping to hear what God has to say about that man in your life, hold the physical reins. Quiet the shouts of your flesh so you can hear the whispers of the Holy Spirit.

Just where is the line?

A good rule of thumb: if it's something you'd suddenly stop doing if Jesus walked into the room, you probably shouldn't be doing it. <u>The reality is: if you're a believer, Jesus is always in the room. Respect His presence at all times.</u> Especially in this very tempting arena where so many have struggled, it's important to be responsive to the Holy Spirit's call to purity, something He knows is best for your growing relationship.

Again, this is not meant to heap condemnation on those who have fallen short. If that's you, know that there is forgiveness for the repentant. You can also ask the Lord to help you recalibrate and start fresh. You can talk about it and agree to help each other to be strong.

Truth be told, there is nothing more intimate or revealing than going before the Almighty in prayer. Prayer is a great intimacy God welcomes you to enjoy together at any point in your relationship. Prayer invites the Holy Spirit into your circle. He will not only give you all the self-control that you will need to resist temptation, but He will also teach you how to rightly relate to each other.

When God does speak, sovereignly bringing two people together, it is with kingdom-building purpose. If you really are a match made in heaven, you'll both be eager to spend time seeking Him about just what purposes you might serve as a couple. The more you resist the flesh and give way to the Spirit, the sharper your ears will be to hear what God is really saying to you about that special man in your life.

FIVE

How God Helps Sort the Laundry

"And just as they did not see fit to acknowledge God any longer, God gave them up to a depraved mind, to do those things which are not proper; being filled with all unrighteousness, wickedness, greed, malice; full of envy, murder, strife, deceit, malice; they are gossips, slanderers, haters of God, insolent, arrogant, boastful, inventors of evil, disobedient to parents, untrustworthy, unloving, unmerciful."

Romans 1:28–31

Talk about a runway full of fashion *don'ts!* Anyone who thinks God doesn't give fair warning about the kind of men His daughters shouldn't marry might not be taking this dirty laundry list from Romans into account. Notice that *malice*—the intent to do harm—is listed in two different spots, perhaps for special emphasis.

This is just one of many passages to keep in mind, all helpful in piecing together what God has to say about how the Mr. Wrongs in our lives deck themselves out. These are worldly men who refuse the clean clothes God offers and choose to suit themselves from the enemy's closet instead.

Before we go any farther on this subject, first things first. As we examine such cautionary Worst Dressed Lists, it should be with a humility prompted by a hard look in the mirror. But for the amazing grace of God, we are all Mr. and Ms. Wrongs. Were it not for the cleansing blood of Jesus, every last one of us would still be piled up in that same grimy laundry basket.

Nothing in this book should be construed to mean that believers should be judgmental. To do so would be to don the unbecoming robes of a Pharisee (Luke 18:10–14).

We should always have Christ-like compassion for those who fall short of the glory of God or who reject the Gospel altogether. Let's remember we probably have a log or two to extract from our own eyes before we get too focused on the specks in someone else's.

It's not about using the Bible to make ourselves feel superior or to shorten the list of people we'll reach out to in the normal course of life. As recipients of God's grace we should be salt and light, mingling with non-believers regularly, the way Jesus did. However, Scripture is clear that there's a difference between associating with non-believers and entering into the covenant of marriage with one.

Marriage is where God, in His mercy, asks us to draw the line. It's your holy get-out-of-jail-free card. It's an instruction our protective heavenly Father makes in His beloved daughters' very best interests.

It's not that you have to find a man who is literally perfect (good thing, because you won't). Just like you, at best, he'll be a sinner saved by grace. Nobody has lived a perfect life except Jesus. But there really is a difference between a godly man who purposes to put on the white robes of Christ each day and a man who sports the enemy's threads as a matter of course.

Clothes that Make the Man

The Bible has a lot to say about the figurative apparel a person may wear. Psalm 73:6 calls pride "*a chain about the neck*" of wicked men. It says that they cover themselves with violence "*as a garment.*" Paul's admonition against lazy men accessorizes with Proverbs' cautionary wisdom that *"drowsiness will clothe a man with rags"* (Proverbs 23:21).

King David cites the boomerang effect when a man clothes himself with cursing as a garment (Psalm 109:17–18). Solomon's wisdom spotlights the fabric of the unfaithful and warns against those who dress themselves with anger and jealousy (Proverbs 22:24, 27:4). In fact, the whole book of Proverbs is a veritable laundry list of applicable comparisons, incredibly useful for sorting between men clad with good or bad character. The list goes on and on. Both the Old and New Testaments are replete with sound Fatherly advice for hopeful brides who have ears to hear.

Alterations

Though some are inexplicably attracted to the "bad boys" among us, it's not that most believing women would actively seek these men as husband material. Nonetheless, despite Mr. Wrong's woefully unattractive style, there is something in us that can still be drawn to these dark, brooding men. Maybe it's our maternal instincts. Maybe we see their torn-up hearts and think a nip and a tuck from us can mend them. We rationalize that nobody's perfect. We hope that the love of a good woman can tailor them to fit, but real change takes so much more than that.

It's not that people can't change. It just doesn't come easily. (It doesn't even come usually.) But people who really want to change can and do, especially those who are truly clothed by the Holy Spirit. It's just that changing for the better can be nearly impossible in the ranks of Mr. Wrongs, and the last person he wants to change him is his wife.

It takes a miracle to change a heart, and God can do it. But as long as Mr. Wrong pushes God away and insists on wearing the enemy's fatigues, he'll stay as he is or get worse. His abusive rages, his compulsive gambling, his laziness, his unfaithfulness, his hatefulness, his addictions—whatever the stronghold in his life—it usually just escalates from the moment his rented tux gets returned after the wedding.

I've listened to the cries of desperate women who married men like this, staking their futures on a *season* of good behavior. No matter how he looks, no matter how in love you are—know this, Dear Sister: Unless he is tamed by the Spirit of God, a wolf is a wolf is a wolf.

He may lure you into a false sense that he's changing his attire; he may make a thousand promises, even that he'll try going to church with you. But in time, his unredeemed nature will get the better of him, and he will strip down to his animal instincts. That's why our heavenly Father gives His daughters fair warning about men of bad character in Scripture. He sees where these men are heading, and the last thing He wants is for one of his precious girls to get trapped into going there.

Checking the Lining

You might find all of this laundry sorting to be a no-brainer. You may have no designs whatsoever upon a Mr. Wrong. His snakeskin couldn't be farther from your style. So, why does the Bible keep calling our attention to clothing?

While spiritual adornment reveals the truth of the heart, earthly clothing covers. It hides what's really underneath. Contrary to conventional wisdom, not every man is what he wears. Take a look back at Paul's list of grimy characteristics: these men are often masters of deceit. They are inventors of evil who are false to the core. They are dressed by the father of lies. Take a gander at Galatians' list of what can be lurking underneath that expensive suit:

"Now the works of the flesh are evident, which are: immorality, impurity, sensuality, idolatry, sorcery, enmities, strife, jealousies, outbursts of anger, disputes, dissentions, factions, envyings, drunkenness, carousings, and things like these: of which I forewarn you just as I forewarned you, that those who practice such things shall not inherit the kingdom of God."

Galatians 5:19–21

Sheep Skins

Many of these deceitful sorts run far outside believers' circles, but Jesus' frank assessments of the inward condition of many religious people also serves as fair warning. In Luke 20:46, Jesus advised wariness of even the religious elite, those who loved to fashion themselves in the respected robes of the pious. In verse 27, Jesus rose to the defense of women when He charged that these men devour the houses of widows. Jesus alerted that false prophets (those who claim to represent God but don't) were like wolves in sheep's clothing (Matthew 7:15).

Long ago, our Good Shepherd said He was sending us out as lambs in the midst of wolves (Luke 10:3). The problem is, wolves don't always look like wolves—at least at first and sometimes for a very long while. They may be covered in fleece. The Bible cautions us to be wary of these deceivers. Paul warned that it should be no surprise to us if even Satan disguised himself as an angel of light (II Corinthians 11:14).

These men who claim to represent God but don't are quite practiced in cunningly costuming themselves as sheep. They may look and talk like the redeemed, but all the while they stalk and win a woman's heart. They carefully conceal what they really are, often until it's too late. It's not at all unusual for a wolf to keep up sheep-like appearances throughout dating and engagement, and then to drop his mask on an unsuspecting bride, only after the wedding has buttoned up her commitment.

It's not that I'm trying to scare you. What I'm encouraging you to do is to be discerning. Listen to what your Father says through His Word. These sometimes hard-to-hear truths can help you look beyond slick exteriors to the heart of that man you're considering, even if he claims to be among the fold.

Heavenly Garments

The good news is that our loving Father has not abandoned us to sort through the laundry unassisted.

In fact, He's promised to send the Holy Spirit as our Helper, to clothe us with the power we need to distinguish what kind of spirit is dressing which man. Just as Jesus was empowered to discern those of good and bad character (John 1:47), the indwelling Holy Spirit is there to manifest that needed gift of discernment in believing women today. Whereas dapper duds may dazzle the natural eye, the Holy Spirit outfits believers to see beyond exteriors and into the heart.

As detailed in my book, *THE HOLY SPIRIT: Amazing Power for Everyday People*, the primary purpose of spiritual gifts is to equip us for service as witnesses. Hear me when I say that this is not about co-opting God's gifts just to screen prospective mates.

That understood, a woman who is filled with the Holy Spirit is more than welcome to pray for discernment regarding the life-altering choice of a husband. After all, it's a choice that can greatly complement or compromise a woman's ability to follow and serve God herself. Life can be a battle, so the value of a husband who puts on the full armor of God should never be underestimated (Ephesians 6:13–17).

In Deuteronomy 30:19, God says that He sets a literal life or death choice before us—a blessing or a curse. The fact is that Mr. Wrongs habitually choose death. Their wardrobes are full of funeral attire. Though the blessing of Jesus' finery is an available option, from the core of their darkened hearts they reflexively choose the couture of the curse. God loves us so much. He wants so much better for His daughters. He wants us to choose life ourselves, and then to share that life with a man who will choose life with us.

Just what does it look like to choose life and blessing? God says it looks like this:

> *"..So choose life in order that you may live, you and your descendants, by loving the Lord your God, by obeying His voice, and by holding fast to Him; for this is your life and the length of your days."*
>
> *Deuteronomy 30:19–20*

Choose life, Daughter of God. Choose the man God is saying He wants for you—a man whose character is fashioned by grace. Choose a man whose heart, soul, mind, and strength are adorned with a passion for God. Choose a man who will love you like Christ loves the Church, a man who is willing to lay down the very life God gives him for the sake of his cherished bride.

That Missing Sock

Finding an M.I.A. spouse can seem like a never-ending laundry day. You've sorted, washed, dried, and folded your clothes diligently. Nothing turned out pink. You'd think the job would be done. But a perplexing thing happens when you go to pair the socks—you know, those pesky, made-for-each other items that seem useless without a mate. Wouldn't you know it? There's an odd one staring you in the face. As lone sock puppets tend to do, it cries out insistently, *"Hey! Where's my partner?"*

You dutifully retrace your steps. You return to the scene of the crime. You run down likely culprits—that wet washer wall or that clingy dryer drum—searching for that sock-mate. If it's not there, you wonder where in the world it could be. Maybe I'm not the only one who has found a lost sock in the last place I look: in the bottom of the laundry basket, right where I left it.

Sock pairs are one thing. They're inanimate attire, just another reminder of the much greater need you may be feeling for your soul-mate. But where do you go to find that missing spouse, that man custom-made to go with you?

Once again, Ruth can serve as a great example. In Chapter One of Ruth, we see that Ruth made a pivotal choice. Actually, Naomi had two widowed daughters-in-law when she left Moab. Naomi urged both Ruth and Orpah to stay in their native land, among their own people, where their prospects for remarrying seemed greater. It was a place that served other gods, but there were many men there. Though they parted with tears, Orpah chose to stay in Moab. In contrast, Ruth took a resolute step of faith. She not only followed her beloved mother-in-law into the land of Judah, she also committed to serve Naomi's God.

Ruth traveled with Naomi to Bethlehem. Reading onward in her story, we learn that it was there where she began to glean in the fields of Boaz. Her selection of fields may have seemed random, but the God she had already chosen was guiding her path, even when she didn't know it. <u>It was in the course of devoted service that Ruth found the love of a truly good man.</u> He was a man who spread his protective covering over her and filled her cloak with provision.

When a woman longs for that perfect pairing, she's faced with a choice, just as Ruth and Orpah were. Like Orpah, she can choose to rummage through familiar, worldly settings, those that seem more densely populated by men. She can search places that serve other gods. In the alternative, she can take a step of faith, as Ruth did. She can venture into the fields of the faithful, trusting that she will find favor with any man God truly wants her to find there. What does all of this have to do with finding that missing sock?

Location, location, location.

It's about being in the center of God's will, that place where God knows you'll meet up with all that He has planned for you. There's no need to obsess over if, where, or when a particular place of intersection will come to be. It could be at work. It could be at church. It could be in your neighborhood soup kitchen. It could even be in that too-long line at the Post Office. If two people who are meant to marry are following God, He'll arrange for them to find each other somewhere along the way.

You don't have to make a made-in-heaven match happen, any more than Ruth did. Just follow Jesus. Glean from the fields of the family of God and trust that He will lead you into everything He has for you. In choosing what seemed the narrower road, Ruth walked straight into God's best. She didn't have to set it up, scope it out, or manipulate it in any way. She simply followed God and found her husband along that divinely lit path.

You won't find socks in Ruth's love story, but footwear definitely came into play. Boaz wanted to marry Ruth, but he was honor-bound to first offer a closer kinsman the opportunity to wed her and to buy the land that she stood to inherit from Naomi. Wisely, Boaz called ten elders of the city to witness his offer. Boaz told the closer kinsman that he would sell him the land, only if he would agree to marry Ruth.

Again, customs were different. In Israel, an offer to marry was refused in this way: the refuser would remove just one of his sandals, and then give it to the man whose offer he had refused. As strange as it may seem, Boaz accepted a worn sandal to seal his right to marry Ruth. That odd shoe stood as a symbol that, while one man declined the pairing with Ruth, Boaz had lawfully accepted it. From that day forward, Boaz was The One for Ruth, as she was for him.

In the loving arms of her kinsman redeemer, Ruth found her place in history, in the lineage of the coming Messiah, who would be born in Bethlehem, as the Redeemer of the whole world.

Making Your Lists and Checking Them Twice

Glad to set the dirty laundry aside? Smile. It's time to sort through the good basket.

While we're on the subject of laundry lists—ever made one of those lists of what you want in a husband? Many such lists have two columns. The first column is that woman's "Must Be" list, those attributes she can't live without. The second column details her "Can't Be" list, reminding her of negative traits she knows she can't abide long-term.

For most women, a third column is formed subconsciously. This list cites those truths a woman hides from herself, those things the soulish part of her wants in a man, even though she can't admit it on paper, to God, or even to herself. It's a list chock-full of wildly alluring physical and material characteristics that can very easily trump her better judgment.

Whether these lists are just in our minds or typed and tacked to our walls, when it comes down to choosing a spouse, all marriage-minded singles make them. Some lists are short and others quite extensive, but no matter the length, all three lists are running in the background every time an eligible man enters the picture.

If a woman is looking to marry, from the instant an eligible man is introduced, this process of evaluation begins.

A very nice believer asked my friend, Paula, out. Lovely and single, Paula was impressed that this man treated the evening as an actual date, right from the start.

So far, so good, right?

As they conversed over dinner, Paula's internal lists came into play. They helped her to evaluate the possibilities as meaningful differences became apparent. The more they talked, Paula realized that some of this man's beliefs were poles apart from hers. As attractive as he was and much as she enjoyed his attentions, she realized they weren't very compatible on a spiritual level. Though he asked to see Paula again, I admired the fact that she stuck to her well-considered convictions and declined.

For some it may seem that marrying within the faith offers a wide variety of choices. Others, particularly those who are older, may think the pickings look pretty slim, tempting those women to adjust their Must Be lists, at times to their peril. Though some Must Be items (like "Must Be a believer") should be in ink, some editing of less essential items on these lists can serve a good purpose. As we mature, we realize that godly character is of much more value than physical or material attributes. In the context of prospective marriage, our eyes are opened to see that qualities like kindness and loyalty are much more attractive than broad shoulders or a great car.

Consider His Character

Think about the things that draw you to whatever man has captured your heart.

Is it his smile, his charm, his good looks, or strong physique? Is he a man of substance, a man of integrity? Does he have a strong work ethic? Is it his personal relationship with God that stirs your interest?

This isn't an invitation to judge your brother in any negative way. I'm asking you to think about his positive qualities. The fact that nobody's perfect, including whoever you've got your eye on, is a given. Everybody has their "stuff," those bits of not-so-attractive baggage we have to accept along with the package deal of who a person is, the same way we hope he'll accept our "stuff" along with who we are.

Okay, enough about his "stuff."

Take a moment and think about the good things about him. Resist the urge to focus on flaws. Just make a list—long or short—of all the good things. Write down the specifics of how he really shines in your eyes under three column headings:

PHYSICAL, PRACTICAL, and SPIRITUAL.

Does he have a great sense of humor? Are his eyes to-die-for? List any physical or intellectual attributes under PHYSICAL. Don't shy away from noting whatever honestly appeals to you about him.

Does he work hard, live within his means, pay his bills and taxes on time? Is he dependable? Does he have a knack for fixing things? Can he cook? Does he keep his living spaces clean? Is he a motivated self-starter? Put those things under PRACTICAL.

Under SPIRITUAL, go beyond the general. You may cite that he's a believer at the top of your list, but also list specifics of how his spiritual commitment actively manifests in his everyday life. Understand that his emotional strengths are a reflection of his spiritual condition.

Think more in terms of listing what he does than what he says about himself. Is he faithful? Does he deal well with stress? Is he even-tempered? Does he tell the truth, even when it's difficult? Would you say he is a kind person? Is he respectful of his mother? Is he patient with children? Will he go out of his way to help a friend, or even a stranger? Is he honest, generous? Does he go beyond simply attending church to giving of his time in service? Is he an avid Bible reader? Is he a good listener? Would you call him a people-person? Write it all down, every attractive spiritual quality you can think of about him.

Resist the urge to read on until you have charted all of his most attractive Physical, Practical, and

Spiritual Attributes. Assuming that you are interested in this man, taking the time to write down his qualities should be a pleasure!

Finished?

Now, take a look at the way your overall charting of attributes is weighted. Does it look fairly even between the three headings, or does one heading or another stand out to you? It may give you insight into which aspect is most important to you in a man.

Let's be honest and admit that physical attraction is a factor and practical considerations are important to consider. But you guessed it—when it comes to what your heavenly Father wants for you, His precious daughter, it's the spiritual category that should carry the most weight.

Take a look at the following passage alongside your list of attributes:

> *"But the fruit of the Spirit is love, joy, peace, patience, kindness, goodness, faithfulness, gentleness, self-control; against such things there is no law."*
>
> *Galatians 5:22–23*

Highlight the spiritual attributes you have already noted that demonstrate any of the fruits of the Holy Spirit in his life. If seeing a particular fruit of the Spirit reminds you of an attribute that you forgot to list, feel free to add it on as long as it's really true of that man. You can check through I Corinthians 13:4–8a for additional ideas of what a truly loving man is like.

Scripture really can help us to get a good picture of what type of man God is saying that He wants for His daughters. They are more than men who just say they believe in God. (After all, James 2:19 says that even the demons believe in God and shudder.) God wants a man for you who goes beyond simple assent to God's existence. He wants a man who is committed to following Christ with his whole heart.

Spiritual attributes are not hard to think of when it comes to true followers of Jesus. They are clothed in the power of the Holy Spirit and they wear the fruit of that fullness, both in and out of season. They are among the true sheep that hear and follow the Good Shepherd's voice.

Know this: If he's a guy God is suggesting as a good choice for you, he is a man who talks to God. He's a man who listens for whatever God might say back to him, even about the choice of a spouse. He's a man who would be willing to pray about what place you might hold in his life. He is also man enough to be honest with you about how he feels.

There are those of you who were tracking with me about that guy you have in mind, right up until the final sentence of the previous paragraph. Your list of this man's spiritual attributes may be overflowing. He's totally available and in the right laundry basket, no doubt. You may have already braved the D.T.R. talk with him, but the question that still remains hanging is: how does he really feel about your potential beyond the close platonic friendship you've been enjoying? If that's you, turn the page.

SIX

Kicking the Best Friend Habit

*"The wings of the ostrich wave proudly; but
are they the pinions and plumage of love?"*
Job 39:13 ASV

Not long after meeting Ryan at church, Paula's phone began to ring on a very regular basis. At last, a spiritually compatible guy was calling!

Paula was delighted by the attentions of this newly available man. There was some talk of his recent break-up, but for the most part, Ryan's calls were focused on getting to know Paula. He'd ask about her day; he'd charmingly acknowledge how much he was enjoying their special friendship. Sometimes they'd talk about faith, music, even politics—anything and everything. Some days he called for no other reason than to enjoy the pleasure of her company. It wasn't long before an attachment began to form in Paula's heart, given what seemed to be promising signals.

You've probably seen those programs on TV. You know, the ones that depict all the elaborate ways males of various animal species strut their stuff to snag a mate. It's fascinating to watch the way God created male animals to communicate their interest. They puff up their chests, dance, turn bright colors, sound off, knock horns, and circle close to those they aim to impress. They boldly stake their claim on a female, defending her against other potential suitors.

There's no question. When a male animal does certain things, the female knows he is declaring himself as a suitor. She's as hard-wired to respond to his advances as he is to make them.

Men have no less distinctive ways of attracting the attention of women.

And attract attention they do.

Bonds quickly form in a woman's heart when a man sends out these signals, the most addictive of which is simply spending time with her. All too often, women get hooked long before men define their platonic intentions. The quandary for women is just as the book of Job put it thousands of years ago.

In light of rampant waving of plumage, how does a woman know if a man is interested beyond that special friendship he's enjoying with her? How does she hold onto her heart?

In this day, when uncommitted relationships are epidemic, where fewer and fewer Christian men seek to be a husband and provider, especially the older and more accustomed they become to single life, Best Friend Habits have gone off the charts. If it's not already called a disorder it probably should be. It's an imbalance of emotions, a relational co-dependency.

Knock-knock, Who's There?

When an eligible man spends time interacting one-on-one with a single woman—whether or not he intends to—it's as if he knocks on the door of her heart. No joke. From the moment she delights in seeing him there, she is created to consider the romantic possibilities. Repeated contact sends a message: *he likes me.*

She invites him into her heart, longing for that soul-level companionship she was created to desire. The more personal the topics of conversation are, the more invested she becomes in the hope that he'll invite her into his heart, too. Even when he keeps her at arms' length romantically, time with him becomes an oh-so-desirable habit.

It's not that Paula jumped the gun or raced ahead when Ryan first started calling her. But over the course of time, the regularity and duration of his attentions sent signals that were hard to ignore. Naturally, Paula began to look forward to every point of contact. She enjoyed seeing him at church as well as in social settings, but the one-on-one communiqués were what meant the most to her. Each personal exchange fueled Paula's hope that Ryan would soon ask her out on a date. The problem was: he never did. He had taken up a place in her heart without welcoming her into his.

If you've experienced this kind of dysfunctional dynamic, you know it. (*You may be nodding in solidarity with Paula as you read this!*) In this age of delaying marriage far past young adulthood, Best Friend Habits are running rampant—abetted by unwitting women who become addicted.

As with anyone who struggles with an addiction, the first step is to recognize that there's a problem. It wasn't long before Paula realized how dependent upon Ryan's attentions she was becoming. Kicking the Ryan habit wouldn't be easy for Paula, especially when she still found so much about him to be so attractive.

Paula went to the Lord in prayer, asking for help. In response, God gave Paula a brief vision. He showed Paula a picture of Ryan in a decidedly less attractive form. Ryan's looks didn't change in the natural. But as Paula kept that picture in her mind's eye, it helped loosen the hold that Ryan had on her heart. She was able to see past peripheral appeals and accept that Ryan was not The One for her.

Though it was hard for Paula to ask Ryan to stop calling, it helped that it was only an attraction Paula felt. She had caught it in time. It would be much more difficult for my friend, Rachel. Rachel had fallen in love.

Having heard that *"Not now"* so many times as she prayed about her best friend, Keith, Rachel had assumed it meant that he would eventually come to see her as more. She had braved the D.T.R. and was waiting patiently. Keith had become a fixture in her life. He had been there for her during a difficult time. She could count on his regular calls, his emails and texts.

Most of all, it was Keith's prayers that cemented his place in her heart, as spiritual intimacies have a way of doing. They'd worship together on Sunday mornings. There were lunches afterward. They'd talk about everything—everything, that is, except the elephant in the room. Not wanting to push, Rachel gave him more time. Month after month, Rachel found herself hanging onto hope.

How to Know if He's a Habit

Do you have a best friend addiction? Maybe you're not so sure you're hooked. Let's start with some simple diagnostics. Think of that man you've been praying about, that friendship you've been nurturing in the hope that it will one day lead to more. Answer the following questions honestly:

- *Does he treat you like a buddy, not a girlfriend?*

- *Does he mention other women who interest him?*

- *Do just the two of you hang out together often?*

- *Do you exchange playful emails, tweets, posts, or IMs?*

- *Does he call you on the phone regularly?*

- *Do you go out on what he won't call dates?*

- *Do you cook or do other domestic favors for him?*

- *Are you a sounding board for him?*

- *Does he encourage you to be interested in another guy?*

- *Does he confide in you?*

- *Does he pray for you in consistently friendly terms?*

- *Does he dodge defining your relationship?*

- *Does he refer to you as a friend or best friend?*

If you answered *yes* to at even half of these questions, chances are you've got a Best Friend Habit. If most or all of these patterns of behavior describe the dynamic, the symptoms are screaming:

You've got it bad.

Yes, strong marriages are built on compatible friendships. Yes, there are times when a close friendship develops into romance. But more often than not, if the "best friendship" hits a comfy plateau where he seems to make camp—where he's satisfied to keep things platonic—it's not going to develop in the direction you'd hope. He's getting all of the favors, admiration, companionship, and emotional support he needs from you without any of the commitment you long for from him. It'd be called emotional thievery if you weren't consenting.

It's not as if you're sinning against God if you opt to continue in a best-friends-without-benefits relationship. But as the Bible points out, there are some sins we commit against ourselves, like if you do give into allowing a man to enjoy physical benefits outside of marriage.

Maybe he has been frustratingly good about keeping things completely non-physical. Still it's important to realize that emotional and spiritual intimacies can still forge deep-set bonds that can be excruciating to break.

We wait, we hope, as our hearts get more and more entwined, as our worlds revolve more and more around these men who rarely, if ever, come to see us in *that way*.

These are soul ties.

The more we let these uncommitted men get wrapped around our hearts, the more established they become as part of who we are, the more painful they are to sever.

Yes, God may have spoken to you about a certain man, but God also gave that man a trump card called free will—including His blessing to pursue another believer or to remain celibate.

Still wondering if you have a Best Friend Habit to kick? Honestly ask yourself this second set of diagnostic questions:

- *Do my prayers often center on this man?*

- *Do I spent a lot of time thinking about him?*

- *Do I carefully dissect everything he says to me for indications of interest?*

- *Do I fantasize about being married to him?*

- *Do I keep track of where he is and what he's saying when we're in social settings?*

- *Are my conversations with friends mostly about him?*

- *Do I plan my calendar based upon where he'll be?*

- *Have I asked my friends to intercede for him?*

- *Do I ignore his signals that he wants to keep things platonic?*

- *Have I disregarded godly counsel I've received about this relationship?*

- *Do I distance myself from those who don't think he'll ever become romantically interested in me?*

- *Am I embracing what I believe God is saying about this man without confirmation from independent sources?*

- *Do I feel the urge to stop reading this book right now?*

Again, if you answered *yes* on many or all of these questions, my prayer is that God will help you to see that there's a problem. Though it can hurt like crazy, you are never closer to breaking free of a dysfunctional relationship than when you stare it down as you are doing right now.

You may not want this freedom. Every co-dependent recess of your heart may panic at the thought of losing him. The problem is that, when you don't have a man's heart, having him is an illusion. It's a mirage that vanishes whenever you start to get close, and then reappears farther away, only to disappear again. It's a soul-level bait and switch that will never satisfy. He's a code your mind will never crack, a brainteaser with no solution. No matter how many times you go over the logic of it, no matter how carefully you analyze every word that man says to you, it will never add up to a balanced relationship. Your mind will reflexively keep trying to solve, solve, solve the unsolvable, until you resolutely kick the habit he's become to you.

Dear Sister—as good as it feels to have those regular calls, to get those funny texts, or even to just see his face—if you want romantic commitment and he doesn't, you're hurting yourself every single time you perpetuate the pattern. You're delaying the inevitable. You're subconsciously reinforcing what has become a dysfunctional habit, deepening your own heartache, and extending your own loneliness.

I've known a number of women who have waited in vain for many years for that best friend to come around, allowing their hearts to be stolen all the while. I've also known women who have courageously diagnosed these highly dysfunctional relationships for what they are and have been set free from this frustrating cycle. One of them is Rachel.

Yes, Rachel kicked her Best Friend Habit. I hope you know how deeply I admire the steps Rachel has taken. Everything in me is cheering for her. No one likes having to submit to the open-heart surgery this can be, but Rachel did it. No one relishes the pain that goes with recovery, but Rachel braved it.

So can you, Woman of God. So can you.

Relationship Rehab

The reason Best Friend Habits are so hard to kick is because the longer we have one, the deeper engrained that object of our affections can become in our lives. Before long, our whole world revolves around that person. In fact, it's very much like a substance addiction.

We get hooked.

Just as an alcoholic must reach the point of admitting there's a problem and participate in solving it—if you're addicted to an unbalanced relationship, you'll need to take some disciplined steps, too. You can beg God to take him out of your heart, but if you don't cooperate with God by resolutely curtailing behaviors that feed your unhealthy habit, it's like an alcoholic praying to be cured of the disease so she can go back to the bottle. It's time for Relationship Rehab.

If you're serious about breaking free of that man's vortex, I recommend declaring a lengthy fast from any form of one-on-one contact with him. Instead, refocus your desires on building your relationship with God. I'm not saying you should ignore that man or be rude to him if you unavoidably see him in public settings. In fact, you should forgive him and conduct yourself with grace. But, especially at first—as much as your heart will crave little sips of the relationship—know that what seem like harmless sips, quickly give way to thirsty gulps that will soon have you falling off the wagon all over again.

If you give into the temptation to indulge yourself in his calls, his playful IMs, his non-date get-togethers, sitting together in social settings, or lunching at work and the like, you'll soon find yourself right back where you started, needing to detox from him cold turkey all over again. It's like an alcoholic who can't take just one drink.

So, as you ask God to take this man out of your heart, do what Rachel did. Resolve to stop putting him back in there. Commit to God that you'll fast from all forms of one-on-one contact with him. Yes, it will be difficult, especially at first. It's a deep-seated dependency. Weaning yourself of his attentions will be painful. It was excruciating for Rachel, but these were her steps along the path to freedom.

Some women hesitate to pull away from Best Friend-ville when they don't see alternative men on their horizon. The problem with that strategy is that it keeps the woman in a relationship that's going nowhere, occupying her heart in such a way that she can't see other, more fruitful possibilities as they pass her by, supposing she is otherwise involved.

The fact is: if you're marriage-minded and he isn't—you're unequally yoked. You're committed romantically, but he's not. If your heart is ever to get to the place where you are ready to be married to another man, one day, you'll have to get over this one. The attentions you enjoy from a male best friend won't be appropriate once you're committed to someone else.

As much as some might protest, it wouldn't be fair to the man you actually marry that you still see another man as your best friend. It could easily open the door to unfaithfulness, at least on an emotional level. Your husband-to-be will deserve that full place in your heart, so it's a good idea to clear that space for him in advance.

Give yourself time to adjust to life without that man who can't see you as the wife you want to be. Do it as a gift to the man who will. Until you do, this dysfunctional relationship will compromise your potential with other men. Worse yet, it could also impede your relationship with God.

When a best friend has become an idol in a believing woman's heart, God has been known to hit the holy hold button. Nothing seems to move forward as God waits to be restored to His rightful place of Lordship in that woman's life.

Think of how long Israel tromped in circles around the wilderness, without being allowed to enter the Promised Land. You may think you've been patient, but you can't out-wait God. Even more than an earthly father waits up for his daughter to return from a date, your heavenly Father will wait up for you to leave that man's company and truly come home to Him.

You may have been crying out to God for this man day and night—even fasting—bewildered that the heavens seem closed to your petitions. But though your Father will not always give you everything you want (*what good father would?*), He will always give you exactly what you need—even if it's a time-out to refocus on your relationship with Him.

Want to know something wonderful about our God? Even when we've wandered in these ways, even when we've allowed our hearts to be stolen, we come home to a compassionate heavenly Father who understands. He's there to dry your tears. He stands ready to respond the moment you ask Him to help you cut the cords that have been binding you.

If that's you and you want to be free of your Best Friend Habit, just reach out to God and say so. Let Him strengthen you to do what may seem impossible. He will help you break every yoke of bondage, every step of the way, just as He's helped my friends, Rachel and Paula, and so many others like them.

When you're ready, take whatever steps you can to readjust your priorities. Think about your emotional triggers. Your to-do list will depend upon the ways you've been dependent. In the same way a recovering addict clears her home of addictive substances, clear your home of photos, mementos, and patterns that keep your heart hooked. Rule of thumb: if it's hard for you to toss that trinket or cancel that non-date, that means you should.

Tackle your technology triggers. Start by dropping his social networking feed. As tempting as it may be to check up on him, to keep following his posts and the like, know it just makes it harder for you to do what you must. Delete your bookmarks to his web pages. Make it harder to reflexively respond to him. Take him off speed-dial. Screen your calls and resist the urge to pick up when he rings. Set up your online presence as invisible so as not to inadvertently encourage spontaneous e-chatting.

Once all of your emotional triggers are neutralized, it's time to be honest and direct with that man in your life. Explain that you realize you need significant time apart from him. Confess that, while you've enjoyed his friendship, you've come to want more than he seems to want out of it. Say that you only want this kind of close friendship with a man who is interested in pursuing you romantically. Tell him you need to clear space in your heart for God to do a new thing. Ask him to refrain from contacting you outside group settings. Even within group settings, ask him to limit personal exchanges with you. Tell him that you'll do the same. Say your goodbyes.

As difficult as it may seem to do these things, it will actually start to feel like a good burn. You'll sense the fire of the Holy Spirit strengthening you. Each time you resist, you'll know you're doing something better for yourself as well as for your eventual husband-to-be. Step out in faith, Sister. Feel that good burn.

The reason that taking these steps feels so empowering is that something in you realizes that you are no longer giving that man control of your life. You are taking control back and giving it over to God.

It can be an emotional roller coaster, absolutely. You may weep your way through it, but that weeping won't go on forever. Know that your Champion is at your side, and that the joy of freedom is coming.

Expect a Challenge

Because I've walked through this scenario with a number of women, I cautioned Rachel about what to expect after she kicked the Best Friend Habit. I told her to expect a challenge.

Sure enough—the next Sunday, there were challenges for Rachel on multiple fronts.

Since there were so many emotional triggers at the church Rachel attended, it was helpful for her to find another place of worship. At first, this seemed to compound Rachel's heartache. Kicking her Best Friend Habit meant walking away from what had been her church home, but still Rachel did it. Not everyone will need to find a new church, but Rachel knew that she would. She wasn't walking away from God. She was walking hand-in-hand *with* God to another body of believers. It was a step of faith that has been greatly blessed.

Anticipate that you'll get a reaction when you cut dysfunctional best friend ties. That man is used to the patterns you've developed. He's accustomed to your attentions, too. He'll likely protest, attempting to draw you back into the way things were. He may even turn up the charm or play on your sympathies. These attempts to re-engage you will likely be repeated over time.

Hold the line in faith.

Do not re-engage.

Politely enlist this man's help in stepping back from the relationship. Be honest and mature enough to admit that your feelings for one another are different. Tell him that you respect his right to not to pursue you, and that you'd like him to respect your need for time apart to move on and heal.

If he asks how long it will be before he can resume personal contact, let him know that you'd only like to hear from him one-on-one again *if* he is ready to seriously pursue you at a time you happen to be unattached. The truth is, if you've been like best friends, he already has all the information he needs to know if he'd ever want to choose you. It's not like another lap around Best Friend Land will seal the deal. So, draw boundaries, say goodbye, cross the border, and don't look back.

Even months after you initiate this fast from contact, be on the alert. Though he may not desire you romantically, he will likely still miss your presence in his life. On a subconscious level, he may even miss the idea that you want him, enough to try and rekindle your passions.

Be on guard if he asks to talk to you privately or sends even a simple personal greeting. This may come weeks, even months later. He is testing your receptivity to return to that Best Friend Habit. If his post makes your heart skip the tiniest beat, know you're not over him. See that casual note for what it is, a challenge to your resolve. It's that one drink an addict must know she can't have. It's the enemy returning at a more opportune time (Luke 4:13).

Prepare yourself for the possibility that he may contact you about something that may tug at your heart. He may have lost his job. He may have gotten a big promotion. A family member may have fallen ill. He may be beside himself, legitimately longing for the comfort of a friend. Maybe he sent you a sentimental birthday greeting. Perhaps he won a contest. It's not that he's necessarily creating these emotional highs and lows to manipulate you, but they will definitely yank at your resolve. They will tempt you to resume your place as his go-to cheerleader or emotional supporter. And if you do, your heart will quickly revert to square one with him.

It's not that you should be heartless if problems come his way. But it's important to realize that sorrows, joys, and special days are the stuff of life. They are the "for better or for worse" that husbands and wives commit to go through together. If you're there for him the way a wife should be, he probably won't feel his need for an actual wife as acutely as God may want him to feel it. There are some times that pangs of loneliness do a good work in us. They can motivate a man to get over any commitment issues he may have and to go about the process of finding a wife, something Proverbs 18:22 says is a *"good thing"* for him.

So, what do you do if you find out his dog died, that he had a car accident, or he's just plain depressed without you? You do what a believer who is just a friend to a guy should do. You pray for him, privately. You entrust him to God's care.

If he's weathering a death in the family, a card with a brief note from you is certainly appropriate. If you're in town, you might attend the funeral without lingering for one-on-one conversation. If a relative of his that you know is hospitalized, you can send flowers or a card straight to that person. Bottom line is: you behave like a friend. Not a best friend. Not a hopeful girlfriend. You can care from arms' length.

Know this: everything in you that's addicted to that man will cry out to you to make an exception, to race to his rescue and to comfort him. You will rationalize that the circumstances are dire. You'll tell yourself that any real friend would become more personally involved. You'll reason that you'll just get him through the next couple of weeks. If you don't resist the pull of those soul ties, they will lasso around your neck and draw you right back into that lopsided Best Friend Habit. You'll compromise your own recovery and end up having to start all over again.

At least until you are completely over him, a good policy to uphold is that the only personal contact you'll respond to from him is an invitation to go out on a real date. As mentioned, it's fine for you to let him know that he's welcome to call you personally, that is, if he should ever get to the point where he'd like to pursue you intentionally. This has been known to happen.

A man who finds himself bereft of a female best friend usually does one of three things:

1. He attempts to get her back as a best friend.

2. He finds another woman to take her place.

3. He misses her so much that he realizes he loves her in ways he hadn't known before she stopped pursuing him.

The latter response is probably by far the most rare; however, when it happens, it's brought about by the space you need to give him. It's that same space and time apart you also need for yourself.

Still hanging in there with me?

God bless you, if you are. Facing up to the hard truths of what God may be saying to you about a Best Friend Habit is a very courageous step to take. It's also the first step toward healing. Know that your Father in heaven wants better for His daughters. He will take your hand and lead you out of this painful place, if you are willing to leave it.

SEVEN

Healing for the Heartsick

"Hope deferred makes the heart sick; but desire fulfilled is a tree of life."
                                         Proverbs 13:12

This is not an easy chapter.

Though it is my fervent hope that many will read this book with joy, my heart goes out to those of you who will read it with tears. I feel just as much for those who will shake their heads in denial, even those who would like to fling this book across the room in anger. These are all valid steps along the pathway to healing, that place a woman reaches when something in her stirs to the impending reality that her dreams of a much-desired man must die.

Especially in this age when nuptials are widely delayed, the aisle to the altar can be long and strewn with shattered emotions. Solomon really got it right when he said that deferred hope makes our hearts sick. When it's marriage a woman is waiting for, adding a ticking biological clock to the equation only amplifies an ache that seems beyond means of treatment. Just like a patient who is told he needs open-heart surgery, it's daunting to think that it has to get worse for a while before it can begin to get better.

There's no getting around the loss it can be to experience unrequited love. No matter the form a break-up takes—whether or not a man ever shared a woman's affections—it's grief, plain and simple. No doubt about it, when a woman invests her heart in a relationship with a man who does not see her the same way, it can be devastating. How great a loss it is depends upon how much and how long she's banked on this particular hope. It really can be a kind of grief that must be weathered, and grieving takes time.

Some might balk at comparing the loss of a man who never returned a woman's affections to physical death. I hear you. It can be undeniably excruciating to mourn the loss of a loved one who will never return. But the same permanence that makes death so very difficult to accept also assists in the grieving process by offering a certain point of closure.

As painful as the physically deceased are to mourn, closure has its benefits. It helps us to move on to know there's no chance of reversal.

Admittedly, it can be infinitely more difficult to weather the loss of an actual spouse. But grieving the loss of an unrequited love does carry its own particular challenge, in that the man a woman has set her hopes upon is still physically alive and able to choose her, and yet he does not. This sends her into a perhaps lesser form of grief, but it is grief, nonetheless.

Mourning begins on a soul level.

Say It Isn't So

Whether a woman loses a beau or a man she'd hoped would be one, it's a heart-level change of life's course. It's a breakup, a disruption of desire. When that breakup is unwanted, it can take a while to come to grips with the fact that it's really over. She can't turn off the "love switch" and it's baffling to think that he can. Her solution: she refuses to accept that the relationship has permanently changed. She comforts herself by imagining that he'll come around one day.

Even if a man has always made his lack of romantic interest perfectly clear, denial can still be part of a woman's process. She grapples with God over him. She surmises that the man must not know his own heart well enough to realize what she means to him.

As long as that man is alive and unmarried, closure can elude her.

A woman's heart's desires wrestle mightily with conflicting realities, begging her to keep pursuing that man, to persist in prayer. She convinces herself that if she'll just hang in there a little longer, that man will surely come to his senses and realize what he's missing in her. He'll resume (or initiate) that romantic relationship she desires.

Meanwhile, she wanders what seems endlessly in the wilderness of unrequited devotion she's invested in far too deeply to abandon. Besides, she reasons, there's no one else on the horizon.

How long a woman stays in this place of denial varies. It's not that her heavenly Father abandons her in this state. Just as God was there as the Israelites blamed Him for abandoning them in the wilderness, God's abiding presence is with those who linger in the desert of disbelief. We may want to go back to Egypt, but He waits to lead us into acceptance of the truth, then onward with life.

Have I Got a Deal for You!

About the time a woman comes to grips with the reality that her possibilities with a man are going south, she may reflexively kick into talk of a trade. She fasts for that relationship. She volunteers, hoping to oblige the Almighty with her good deeds. She plunks down promises from Scripture like cosmic coupons she expects to redeem. She prays what seems round the clock. She vows to serve God for life if she can just have that man.

There is some healing value, even as these negotiations continue. As tenacious as she can be in the bargaining process, each refused offer inches her toward what her real bottom line will be. It's not that I recommend these futile attempts to manipulate our Maker. Doing so is about as far from the Gospel of grace as you can get. But desperate hearts take desperate measures.

Eventually, just as a begging child learns from a loving parent that no means no, we learn that it's fruitless to try to strike these deals. It's not that we can earn God's favor or impress Him with all we can offer in return if He'll only give in to us. We can't shame the Almighty into delivering a man He never promised.

No matter how we try to spin it, God won't make a man pursue a particular woman. In time, we come to understand God's refusal to do that as protection and re-direction. Healing progresses as we bow to the superior judgment of our heavenly Father and table these futile pleas.

Adventures in Anger

The range of emotions continues in what can be random order, sometimes skipping or reordering steps. Not everybody goes down this road, but for many rejected women, anger isn't far from the surface. While she may fume at the object of her affections (the man who doesn't see her *that way*), she may also rail at God for refusing to turn that man's heart toward her. She may grouse at her Creator for making her the way He did. She may resent her married friends, just because they have what she doesn't. She may kick herself for falling for the guy in the first place.

Isn't it nice to know that it's possible to be angry and yet not in sin? Anger is a normal human emotion, something even Jesus experienced. Ephesians 4:26 actually encourages us to feel anger, but just as quickly as it does so, it follows with the immediate reminder not to let anger give way to sin.

Ever wonder what biblically-sanctioned anger looks like in a relationship? Where is the line between the non-sin of being angry and the sin that can come from it? There's a clue at the end of that same verse where it is advised that we shouldn't let the sun set on the anger we feel. So, though it's okay to experience the natural emotion of anger, it's not a good place to linger.

Think of anger as if it were the dry seed of a fast-growing weed. If you plant it in a moist, dark place by sleeping on it, before you know it, a root of bitterness begins to grow (Hebrews 12:15). That root spreads out beneath the surface of who you are. It tangles into the core of your being.

The more that anger is watered and fed, the more invasive it becomes. What started out as just a single root branches out underground. It sends out tillers and rhizomes. You may have just planted it in what you thought was a manageable spot, but anger respects no boundaries. Soon, it's popping up here, there, and everywhere. Allowed to remain, it will bear bitter fruit. The supporting root system will continue to grow till it compromises your emotions entirely or until it is completely (and often painfully) dug out.

Experiencing anger can be a very natural part of the loss a woman feels over a man, and she has done nothing wrong to feel it. It's just not something to sleep on or cultivate. It's that root of bitterness that gives birth to sin, and the rotten fruit of angry acts that arise out of it. It leads to backbiting, resentment, retaliation, and unforgiveness.

There's no denying anger. If you feel it, you feel it—and that's okay. Just don't plant that seed. Don't tuck it into the soil of your heart. Communicate instead. The most healing thing you can do with anger is to have an honest heart-to-heart talk about it with your Father. He's that kind of approachable Abba "Daddy" God. When you're hurting, He wants to hear about it. You can tell Him every last detail that upsets you. You wouldn't be the first. Just read the Psalms. You'll see that David vented his anger to God on a regular basis and was still known as a man after God's own heart.

God is saying, *"Come to Me."* Tell Him all about it. Be honest, even if it involves respectfully confessing ways you've been angry with Him. After you've gotten it all off your chest, take a breath or two.

Let your broken heart rest a bit.

Now, picture your Father's right hand of blessing reaching out toward you. Release the seed of that anger into His waiting hand. He knows you needed to vent. He knows you now need somewhere to put your anger seed, somewhere other than the receptive soil of your heart.

Think of it: your anger will never grow into a root of bitterness or yield a single sin as long as you give it over to God unplanted. Even if there's already a massive root-ball, unearth it and give it to Him. It will mark a giant step in your healing process.

There really is a satisfaction that comes with being able to express anger, especially when you can talk it through and leave it with a God who loves you so much. He understands the pain of rejected love acutely. No human being knows better what that's like. He's been weathering that grief since the first man and woman were created. He is the best listening ear you'll ever have, and it is His good pleasure to be a comforting balm to your wounded soul.

So Low about Being Solo

What is it about sadness over singleness that's so isolating? Maybe it's the way it distances a woman from virtually everyone she knows. The last one on earth she wants to see her this way is *that man*.

As much as it kills her, she pulls away from him. She dodges her friends, especially those she fears may judge her. She worries they'll say she was off-base to think that God spoke to her about that man in the first place. This heavy blanket of loss even seems to separate her from herself, as if she's watching a picture of a wilting clone, close enough to observe, but wholly unable to reach.

She sinks into numbing despair. The life fades from her eyes. She struggles for strength just to function, much less recover. She withdraws socially. She eats too little or too much. She snaps at her loved ones' feeble attempts to help. She fumes at her Maker. She bludgeons herself mercilessly, feeling more unattractive and more unworthy of true love than ever.

Wait a minute.

Didn't I say this was a chapter about healing?

Actually, it is. Walking through the valley of sadness is a very meaningful part of the process of grieving the lost hope of an unrequited relationship.

Please keep in mind that this is not a book about overcoming clinical depression, and I am not a physician. If you're fighting clinical depression, then it's a good idea to pray and see a doctor about it as a separate health issue. This is, however, a chapter about dealing with temporary romantic doldrums, the situational sadness that follows dying to the dream of a certain man. If that's where you find yourself, I hope God will use this to comfort your healing heart.

Admittedly, when a woman is mired in the solitude of gloom over the loss of a man, it doesn't feel like much healing is taking place. Life doesn't seem to move ahead in any way. In fact, something in the withdrawal of this state makes it feel like regression. It's as if she's moving backwards, like she is being distanced not only from the man she wanted, but also from everything and everyone else.

There's a numbness that sets in, an inability to fully focus on anything else for a time. Believe it or not, this numbness can be a good thing. Remember how I said that, on an emotional level, losing a hoped-for husband can be a bit like open-heart surgery? It really can be. So, tell me, would you even think about letting a surgeon crack your chest without the assistance of anesthesia?

Never. Nor does your Great Physician allow you to go through the searing pain of loss without helping to lessen it.

2008 was a year of many losses for me. By the end of May one dear friend and four family members passed into eternity, the latter four within the space of two weeks. It's always difficult to lose a loved one, but the hardest passing of all to bear was that of my father. I adored him more than I can express, and even now—years later—my eyes brim as I write this.

It's not that I was pain free. I definitely felt it. It's not that I was unable to function. It's just that God strengthened and sustained me to get through it. Each time, though, I noticed that something of an emotional numbness came over me. It was a numbness I couldn't shake. I could still feel what I was going through, but it didn't seem that I could entirely focus on the latest life-altering loss. There was no pushing through this numbness. I was assured that it was normal, that the fog of grief would lift in time.

Indeed, as the months went on, the isolating haze slowly lifted. Gradually, life found its new normal. Clarity returned. At the time, it had seemed that the numbness delayed my healing, but in retrospect, it seems to have played an important part. It was as if God Himself had been taking the edge off my emotions. When I most needed it, He had softened the repeated blows of pain, and then gradually tapered it off as I became more accustomed to life without those I'd lost. The numbness that seemed limiting at first was actually part of my healing process.

As the weeks turned into months after Rachel cut her ties with Keith, she asked me the same question others have: *"How long is it going to hurt this badly?"*

All I could say was that healing takes time. Just like a deep physical wound, the ache of it would slowly subside. It would get a tiny bit better each day she resisted feeding the dependency.

God was there with Rachel when it hurt the most. He stayed with her as the intense initial pain of it began to subside day by day. It was a time of weeping, but not a single tear fell without her attentive heavenly Father's notice.

> *"Thou hast taken account of my wanderings; put my tears into Thy bottle: are they not in Thy book?"*
>
> *Psalm 56:8*

There are times it seems no bottle could contain the tears and no book could possibly account for all of them. And yet, God is faithful to do just that. Our heavenly Father lovingly tends our wounds, even when we reopen them and set the healing process back.

It may be a long, dark night of your soul, but this verse will be so true of it:

> *"Weeping may last for the night; but a shout of joy comes in the morning."*
>
> *Psalm 30:5*

Maybe you've suffered an emotional loss. Maybe you're sensing that emotional numbness. If you are, thank God for it. Thank Him for putting that natural damper on your pain. Maybe you're staying home more, getting more rest, saying *"no"* to social engagements. It's okay for just a little while, as long as you're taking care of yourself, spending time with the Lord to allow Him to minister to you, and not sinking into clinical depression.

Don't worry that you're not doing enough to make the pain subside. Just rest in your Father's strong arms and let Him carry you through this time. Just as when a person is physically ill, when we suffer an emotional trauma, it can be good to have a certain amount of quiet time.

As far as human company is concerned, you may be alone, but God will never forsake you. You don't have to pretend to feel great. No need for make-up. Just sit with Him like the loving Father that He is.

Know that Jesus is interceding for you (Romans 8:34). You don't even have to talk. Allow the Holy Spirit to express your pain in ways you can't even utter (Romans 8:26). Whether at work or at home, go about your day together.

Let the balm of the following healing verses sink deep into your wounds:

HEALING FOR THE HEARTSICK

"Can a woman forget her nursing child?...Even these may forget, but I will not forget you. Behold, I have inscribed you on the palms of My hands; your walls are continually before Me."

Isaiah 49:15–16

"I have loved you with an everlasting love: therefore I have drawn you with lovingkindness."'

Jeremiah 31:3

"His left hand is under my head, and His right hand doth embrace me."

Song of Solomon 2:6 ASV

"Blessed be the God and Father of our Lord Jesus Christ, the Father of mercies and God of all comfort; who comforts us in all our affliction, so that we may be able to comfort those who are in any affliction with the comfort with which we ourselves are comforted by God."

I Corinthians 1:3–4

> *"Behold, I will do something new; now it will spring forth; will you not be aware of it? I will even make a roadway in the wilderness, rivers in the desert."*
>
> *Isaiah 43:19*

Signing for the Package

Isn't it a little comforting, when Proverbs 13:12 says *hope deferred* makes our hearts sick, that the word *deferred* only indicates a delay rather than an ultimate defeat? It doesn't mean the hope to marry will never be realized; instead, it speaks of a postponement. The Greek word for *deferred* also means *to develop* or *march*, further encouraging us onward toward that *tree of life* ahead, that place where we find satisfaction with God, whether single or married.

If the process of getting over a guy is a likened to a cross-country march, it doesn't seem to follow a straight course or an even grade. There are those strenuous uphill sections where everything in you screams you can't go another step. There are plateaus of rest, those temptations to quit or retreat, those twists and turns of the unexpected, long before that promised tree of life comes into view. Often, we can't see it at all until we round something of a final corner.

Maybe you're still early in the course. You may still be flat out on the operating table with your heart wide open, not up and around at all yet. If so, that's okay. Just know that if you take the hand of help God offers you, one day you'll find yourself turning that corner called acceptance. You'll see the bright future ahead of you, the hope He has promised you.

When will that day come? When will you be out of this wrenching pain? It depends. The details are different for every woman, but many times we begin to turn that corner when we open the door to it. Often, it's long after we begin to hear a soft but persistent knock. This time it's not that man at the door. It's Jesus:

> *"Behold, I stand at the door and knock: if anyone hears My voice and opens the door, I will come in to him, and dine with him, and he with Me."*
>
> *Revelation 3:20*

"Wait a minute," you might say. *"I already opened the door of my heart to Jesus a long time ago. He's actually the only reason I'm surviving this pain; He's the only friend I've got left."* No question—this verse paints a picture of that moment when we first open our door to the Lord, but it's also just as true of God's initial call to

relationship as it is every step along the way of that continuum.

It may be that it's not an exterior door Jesus is knocking on this time. It could be that basement door you've sequestered yourself behind. It may have been a while since you've really supped with Him and received the sustenance He wants to set before you.

It could be that you're not alone in the basement. Maybe no matter how dark and cold it is, you are still harboring hope for that man who rejected you there. You know that letting Jesus come into that position of first-place devotion also means letting that man out of it, once and for all.

So, though you've heard that quiet knocking at that inner door of your heart all along, you haven't been in any hurry to answer it. You know Who's there. You know about the package that's being delivered to you, but you're not ready to open that particularly private door and welcome the Deliverer, much less sign for the package that's been sent. You know Jesus well enough to reason that He'll keep knocking.

When it comes to really giving that man in your life over, it's hard to look Jesus in the eye, harder still to say, *"You, Lord, are my first and greatest love. I trust You to do what's best for me, whatever that may mean."*

These are simple words, but they can be extremely difficult to say and truly mean. The reason it's hard is that they put to death all idols that stand between a woman and her Maker (Revelation 2:4).

This is another one of those points where anger may rise up in some. The last thing you may want to hear is some author who doesn't even know you point out that, ultimately, God is saying that He wants to be The One in your life. It may be that He already is. If so, you may move through this step more easily than most. It may just be the pain of loss and human loneliness that still plague you.

For those who struggle to honestly say those words—*Lord, you are my first love*—it may be helpful to examine what might be compromising your ability to speak them. Ask yourself why you can't say He's first in your heart, that you trust His goodness, no matter what. Let the question stand until you find the answer.

Though some don't dare to admit it, sometimes it's that we're holding out on God, subconsciously challenging Him to give us what we want by showing Him just how much it's hurting us not to have it. It's a back-alley return to the bargaining table.

We throw inner tantrums.

We waste away, threatening spiritual suicide, hoping He'll sympathize and give in to us. We attempt to shame the Almighty, suggesting that He's shirked on His responsibility to provide our longed-for husband, implying that He's not as good as He says He is.

We rationalize that saying "*I trust you to do what's best for me*" is like quitting a hunger strike. We willfully continue the campaign in a vain attempt get our way.

Many times, the reason we can't say *"Lord, I trust you with this"* is simply fear. It's a spirit that didn't come from your heavenly Father. Fear that God won't ever fulfill your desire for a human husband if you agree to blindly trust Him makes it all the more difficult to sign for that package He offers. Understanding, God lovingly continues to knock, never short-selling the fact that He wants to be the Number One love of your life.

> *"For I am jealous for you with a godly jealousy; for I betrothed you to one husband, that to Christ I might present you as a pure virgin."*
>
> *II Corinthians 11:2*

That's right. Over every other person or thing, God wants your unrivaled love. He wants you to fully trust Him concerning all human bonds.

It's not that your relationship with God precludes human marriage. After all, He created and blesses matrimony. He said it wasn't good for people to be alone. It's just that, if you are a believer, above all you have engaged yourself to a heavenly Husband. You are being prepared to be the pure bride of Christ. You may come to marry an earthly man, but until then and even thereafter, these words apply:

> *"For your husband is your Maker; whose name is the Lord of hosts...For the Lord has called you, like a wife forsaken and grieved in spirit, even like a wife of one's youth when she is rejected, says your God."*
> *Isaiah 54:5–6*

The idea of accepting the husbandry of God can be hard to wrap our minds around—much less our arms. It seems almost too exclusive, too intimate a requirement, too much to ask of a woman crying out for a flesh and blood husband. We resist receiving the comfort of these verses, just like we avoid answering Jesus' knock at the door of this particular romantic hideaway. Yet there this passage is in Scripture, awaiting our signature of acceptance on that heavenly marriage license.

If you're struggling with the idea of embracing a type of spiritual betrothal to God, this is one of those times that a peek into the original language can be helpful. When the verse calls God our Husband, the Hebrew word *husband* can mean more than we usually think it does in a human sense. In its spiritual context, it can be translated to mean *Master*, The One who rules over us, The One who possesses us, having bought us with a price. It applies equally to both genders, throughout the Church as His bride.

This isn't a fixed marriage any more than it's a forced one. God proposed to us that we accept His lordship in our lives and those of us who are in Christ have accepted that proposal. Our Maker is our Master and we have willingly given our lives to Him. This commitment to put Him first does nothing to preclude or impede earthly marriage and everything to establish the firm foundation of faith a good earthly marriage can be built upon one day.

As long as we may delay answering, Jesus keeps knocking at that inner door. God loves us faithfully and He doesn't abide the presence of a rival for first place in our hearts. He's not banging the door down, but that knocking you hear will persist till you open the door to that inner room and restore Him to His rightful place as Master of your whole heart.

Once you open the door, look Jesus in the eye, take the whole package He hands you and sign for it, He will come in like the gentleman that He is. He will exude peace and understanding from the moment you accept His presence. Nothing may change in the natural. But on a spiritual level, the clouds will begin to part and the sun will break through as you sit with the Lover of your soul.

You open the package He's brought. Inside you discover that there's a nourishing meal He's prepared, to refresh and strengthen you. You thank Him for being your sustenance. You start to truly sup with Him.

Instead of just talking *to* God, you start talking *with* Him.

You'll pause to listen to what He has to say.

He'll break the bread of life with you, strengthening you with sweet communion. He'll rejuvenate your parched soul with new wine. If you let him, He will begin the work of rebuilding your broken heart, just like the gem of a spiritual Husband that He is.

Tenderly, He'll clear the pieces of your shattered dreams, fully empathizing with the heartache you're feeling. You'll watch as He begins to build anew, just as He promises:

> *"O thou afflicted, tossed with tempest, and not comforted, behold, I will set thy stones in fair colors and lay thy foundations with sapphires."*
>
> *Isaiah 54:11*

You may not feel so very beautiful when this work of restoration begins. But just as the prophet foretold, God will help you clear the debris of devastation and begin to rebuild your life from the very foundation.

Instead of the drab cinderblock used by earthly builders, you'll watch as your heavenly Father sets this new foundation for you in beautifully colored gemstones. In exchange for the ashes of grief, He will wash away your tears and bless you with renewed beauty. God will give you gladness of heart in exchange for the mourning that's been weighing you down. Your weary lips will again find words of thanks and praise (Isaiah 61:3).

True to His Word, God will rebuild your spiritual house—not overnight, but steadily—stone atop precious living stone, resting firmly on the cornerstone of Christ. It may not look like much at first, but see what's coming with the eyes of faith. He will faithfully rebuild your heart into a place of rest, a habitation of peace.

EIGHT

How to Know if He's The One

> *"There are three things which are too wonderful for me, four which I do not understand: the way of an eagle in the sky; the way of a serpent on a rock; the way of a ship in the middle of the sea; and the way of a man with a maid."*
>
> Proverbs 30:18–19

The way of love between a man and a woman is a mystery. It's a wonder even Solomon in all his God-given wisdom never came to understand. There's no formula, no scientific protocol to create the kind of enduring love we deeply desire to find. We don't even fully grasp what it is until we experience it firsthand. But everything in us yearns to solve this mystery, to find that special someone whose heart beats in time with ours.

No matter how long true love eludes us, we continue to search. We watch for clues, run down red herrings, and find out by process of elimination where the answer isn't. What we want takes on greater definition. We linger with persons of interest along the way, investigating the possibilities. Unsure just how much or how little to expect, we turn to our heavenly Father, asking for assurance that we've really found the right guy.

Still waiting for that bolt from the blue about someone you've been dating, maybe a little handwriting in the clouds? Still hoping for clarity from God if that particular guy is The One?

If you're of marriageable age, you've been seeing someone for a considerable length of time, you love each other, and you're still asking God if he's The One, ask yourself why you're hesitating. More often than not, there's a reason.

It may be that your guy hasn't proposed yet. But the farther down the relational road you go, the more you wonder if you're settling for less than you should. Maybe something inside you wants to keep your options open to see if you can do better. Maybe you're not sure if you can live with the challenging aspects of relationship with him long term. And I'll say this as gently as I can for those readers who may find it to be pertinent: maybe something inside you is subconsciously sloughing the question off on the Almighty because you're afraid to make this decision He's given to you.

Perhaps there's been no bolt from the blue, no thundering voice from heaven, not even a whisper to let you know, once and for all, if this man is The One for you. Indeed, there are times when God speaks definitively about a matter, but when He doesn't, it's time to apply what He's already said through His Word, and to use the mind He gave you to make the best choice you can. It can also help to seek biblical counsel from mature believers who may be able to add a more objective viewpoint.

Know that God is not the author of any relational confusion you may feel (I Corinthians 14:33). If you are more confused than peaceful about the choice of a man, wait. No matter how pressed you may feel by circumstances, the expectations of your family and friends, your biological clock, or even a man's desire to marry you, this is not a decision to be made from the pressure-cooker of confusion.

Of course, no human knows just what the future holds, so you'll never be sure of exactly what's ahead. What you do need to be sure of is that, whatever is in store, you are ready to commit absolutely to stand by your choice of a husband.

The Blue-Sky/Gray-Sky Challenge

Whereas romance tends to prompt us to focus on blue-sky projections, the wise take time to honestly assess how the inevitable gray skies of life could impact the choice to marry. If you're on the fence about a guy, it can help to give some practical application to how those general blue-sky/gray-sky promises of the wedding vows could play out in your life together, especially the gray-sky parts that we don't like to think about so much. Don't be concerned that such thoughts will jinx your future. God isn't a jinxer. <u>He wants you to walk in faith, not be paralyzed by superstition.</u> Remember, He actually encourages us to consider the cost of what we embark upon in life, before we do so.

Take an honest look at that man you're considering. What if his work required great spans of time apart *(for better or worse)*? Consider how you would feel about marrying him if he sustained a comprehensive financial loss *(for richer or poorer)*. If you knew today that he would become chronically ill at an early age would you still want to marry him *(in sickness and in health)*? How about if he became unwilling or unable to father children? Would that be a deal-breaker for you?

All too often, it goes like this: a woman is swept up in romance when she believes God is saying a man she desires is The One for her, even more so if the man feels the same way. Gray-sky possibilities are ignored in favor of the much more enticing to contemplate blue-sky potentials. Momentum builds as he returns her affections with a proposal. In a flurry of excitement, they marry. It's bliss—for a while.

In time, as all couples do, they return to the challenges, work, and mounting bills of reality. That honeymoon feeling fades. Life happens.

It's harder than she anticipated in the rush of romance—in fact, romance may disappear from the equation altogether, especially as children enter the picture.

She becomes a sports widow. He feels woefully disrespected. Differences emerge, spurring conflict. Bitterness and resentment creep in through multiple portals. Heated arguments become a matter of course. Terrible things get said. The marriage starts to feel confining, more like a prison than a home. She cries out to God in exasperated anger:

This is Your fault! Why didn't You stop me from marrying him? Why did You say he was The One?

Think how God must feel, taking the brunt of a woman's blame, even though He never forced her to choose that man in the first place. Rather, in His great wisdom, our heavenly Father gives us reasonable parameters, and offers this important choice to us. The responsibility is ours to choose well, and then to live with the "better or worse" of the choices that we, of our own accord, make.

When Opposites Attract

The greater the differences between a man and a woman, the more potential there is for conflict to erupt. Learning to forgive and love each other through the challenges of Oneness builds grace in us, shaping and polishing us in ways that only a marriage can.

It may be that staying married is one of the hardest and most wonderful things you'll ever do. God's Word says that the flesh wages war against the Spirit, and that iron sharpens iron (Proverbs 27:17). No wonder those sparks can start flying! Still, day-to-day in marriage, God says we're modeling the mystical union between Christ and His flawed but forgiven Bride, the Church.

Two believers may be very different in terms of temperament, personality, and what they want in life.

That doesn't mean they can't have a good marriage, but it will likely mean a more difficult one. The ability to resolve conflict in healthy ways becomes essential. The truth is that even the best marriages can be challenging. Many have serious thorns leading up to the roses they produce. That's why we need the mutual love of God to sustain us, especially through the rough patches we'll inevitably hit.

Despite your differences, you may love each other with a passion. You may assume that your love is strong enough to endure the refining fires of marriage. Keep in mind that passionate people are passionate in their expressions of other emotions than love. Both men and women have been known to turn on a loved one with surprising fury. The heat of those blazes can be wildly underestimated, scorching the uninitiated. It makes it all the more important for the staying power of relationships to be tested on the red-hot griddle of real-life conflict.

Fighting Flags

Get ready, Reader. I'm about to make what may be a surprising recommendation to every woman who is contemplating marriage:

Do not accept a man's proposal until you have successfully worked through at least one significant disagreement, better yet a heated argument that leaves at least one of you (preferably both) in tears.

You may say you're in love, that you get along famously, and that you never fight. But if you've never been in the thick of serious conflict resolution with that man, you don't really know him. You don't truly know yourselves as a couple. You haven't experienced what it's really like to be diametrically opposed about something that's truly important to you. Neither of you knows what it's like to hurt the other. You don't know what means the other will resort to in order to win an argument. You don't know if you have the skills to survive the trials of life and forgive.

There are so many things God can say to you in the midst and aftermath of conflict with a potential husband. The fact is, no matter how different or alike you are, conflict will arise in your life. Waiting to resolve a significant conflict before marriage gives God a chance to show you things about each other that you can't see any other way. You may not get an audible word from God about him. But in the aftermath of such a conflict, you may sense God waving a red, yellow, or green flag.

God can speak volumes to you about each other through conflict and the way the two of you resolve it. He can show you whether you face trouble head-on, or if one of you brushes it off in denial. You can see if either one of you has anger management challenges. You'll find out if you talk *with* each other or *at* each other. You'll discover if you're able to listen to each other, or if either of you have the capacity to absorb the other one's differing point of view at all.

Can you compromise? Does he get scary or physical? Do you say hurtful things? Is either one of you a conversational bully? How about a pushover? Would you describe yourselves as gentle or harsh with each other in the midst of an argument? Do you shut each other out, or patiently hang in there till you resolve things? Are you willing to sacrifice for each other? Do both of you have the capacity to forgive?

Frequency of fights can be very revealing. It can be God's way of warning or encouraging you about a man. If you're fighting a lot now, in all likelihood, the frequency and severity of your arguments would increase exponentially in the context of a marriage. On the other hand, if you rarely get into these hurtful exchanges—and when you do, you are able to resolve them and forgive—that could be a promising signal.

So, don't be afraid of asking your guy the hard questions or of getting into an argument prior to the wedding. Don't fear that it will rock the boat. That storm you may have viewed as an attack of the enemy might actually serve a good purpose. God may use it to give you a much-needed window into what life could be like when things aren't so carefree and romantic. It may tell you that you're not as right for each other as you'd thought pre-conflict. On the other hand, you may come out of that storm with the assurance that there is no one on earth you would rather go through the challenges of life with than that particular man.

Couples' Counseling

Still on the fence? Consider couples' counseling. It's another way God might speak to you about that man in your life.

While there are many churches that require premarital counseling after engagement, it can be even better to go through a structured course of counseling once the relationship becomes serious, even before engagement.

Counseling during engagement can be great. Don't get me wrong. I recommend that, too. There's a giant gotcha in waiting until after engagement to seek counseling, though. That gotcha is called the engagement train, and I'm not just referring to the veil a bride may opt to pre-order. I'm talking about the full-steam-ahead locomotive of plans, that chugging engine that leaves the station the moment a proposal of marriage is accepted.

Once the engagement train is running along that track to the wedding, it's a lot harder to disembark. The lure of adventure calls. The spotlight of attention shines on the engaged couple. Gifts begin to arrive. The excitement of the desired destination becomes the focus. Problem-solving skills shift to the complex to-do list, moving rapidly toward the impending nuptials. Bumps along the way are quickly dismissed as the mounting expenses of this preliminary commitment make it increasingly difficult to break. No wonder it's harder to hear God's still, small voice over the roar of that high-speed railroad.

It's understandable that some may resist pre-engagement couples' counseling, preferring to truly pop the question. However, those who'd rather have a proposal of marriage come as a complete surprise may have many more surprises to deal with after the wedding. Now, I'm not saying that every dating couple should take a pre-engagement course or see a couples' counselor, but I do think it can be a great help to couples who are serious enough to start thinking about the possibility of engagement.

For those who don't have affordable access to a pre-engagement counselor, there are a number of good, faith-based workbooks you can go through together, prompting you to make decisions and spot potential incompatibilities, before the pressure of buying a ticket on the engagement train. They'll pose the sometimes hard-to-ask questions and encourage you to come up with honest answers. They'll help you work through those financial issues you're reluctant to discuss. They'll encourage you to be honest with each other about family planning. They'll help you get specific about what you really want in life and just how compatible you are on a spiritual basis.

One reason I recommend these workbooks and/or pre-engagement counseling is that I've known both to either make or break relationships. No matter how it goes, it's for the best. So, open your ears to what God might say to you through these types of resources.

As you begin, you can pray with each other and invite the Holy Spirit to speak to you about whether or not you're well suited for each other. If one or the other of you is unwilling to pray about this (or even to take part), even that should tell you something. For compatible couples, the process of getting to know each other in the nitty-gritty details is a challenging delight. For those not-so-well suited pairings, it just might save them from the heartache of a commitment that never should have been made.

If your man proposes marriage before you've gone through such a workbook or counseling, consider suggesting this kind of guided, purposed exploration before you say *"yes."* It can be an eye-opening reality check as well as an opportunity for God to reveal important things to you about each other, before the often-overwhelming pressure of official engagement.

There is a misconception out there that only those who are weak or in trouble need counselors. It is contrary to the voice of Scripture:

> *"Where there is no counsel, purposes are disappointed; but in the multitude of counselors they are established."*
> *Proverbs 15:22 ASV*

Godly counsel is a good thing. It helps us avoid the disappointing losses of committing to one another in the excitement of romance, before we've really thought through these important decisions as carefully as we should. It's biblically recommended for all who want to hear what God is saying about His purposes in our lives, and about those who may or may not be best suited to help us carry out those purposes. It's for those who need to see that it's best to abandon plans of marriage, and for those who would establish a strong foundation for the future. It can help you to know if that man really could be The One for you.

How To Be Absolutely, Positively Sure He's The One

Though Joseph received rather spectacular confirmation from God that Mary was The One for him, perhaps we can all agree to the exceptional quality of that particular situation. God gives most of us a choice, only asking us to opt within the family of our faith.

We're wise to rank good character and compatibility high on our short lists of non-negotiables—maybe toss in a reasonable level of attraction as a lesser priority. It can be extremely helpful to get to know each other over time as friends, but sooner or later it comes down to the free-will choices men and women are given the privilege to make. Many still long for that know-that-you-know certainty from God that a particular man truly is The One. Believe it or not, it's an assurance you really can have.

Think of it this way: if you go hunting for your dream home, you'll see any number of houses that could potentially fit the bill for you. Maybe the first thing that catches your eye is the curb appeal. But then you walk through the inside; you inspect those aspects that aren't as readily apparent, maybe call in an expert to check the soundness of the foundation. You weigh how suitable a particular dwelling might be to your needs and desires. You imagine what it would be like to spend the rest of your life there. No matter what the real estate agent says, you're the buyer, so you get to make the selection. The moment you commit and sign the deed, that home you've chosen becomes "the one" for you.

Of course, choosing a spouse is far more complex—especially given human emotions and the two-way nature of the choice—but hopefully you get the point. Simply put: if you choose a man who also chooses you, the day the two of you marry, you become The One for each other. From the moment you stand at the altar and pledge your love—yes—God is saying the man you have married is The One for you. God accepts your choice and unites the two of you as One in His eyes.

Maybe you think you've found your soul-mate. Maybe your spirits are in sweet harmony. Maybe you've prayed about it and all systems seem "go."

But how can you be absolutely, positively sure about your choice?

When it comes to the kind of enduring love it takes to live out life as The One for another person—for better or for worse, for richer or poorer, in sickness and health, parted only by death—that reply we get from the happily wed in Christ applies: you just know.

NINE

The Wedding Singer

> *"Jehovah thy God is in the midst of thee, a mighty one who will save; He will rejoice over thee with joy; He will rest in His love; He will joy over thee with singing."*
> *Zephaniah 3:17 ASV*

What is it like when God leads two people together? The stories are as unique as any woman and every bit as lovely. In Chapter Two, I promised you I'd follow up with more of Kelly's story. Kelly realized she'd been mistaken about Tim long ago, but she never stopped believing in the God who spoke to her in such personal ways on other occasions. Though the wait was long, she never stopped trusting God about the husband she so greatly desired.

Do you know what it's like when a fine orchestra warms up? When you hear that sound, you realize that beautiful music is about to begin. That's how it was for Kelly.

Kelly always loved to sing to the Lord, but this particular morning it would not be Kelly doing the singing. It would be a living and active manifestation of Zephaniah 3:17. Just as the verse says, the Lord was with Kelly as she slept, resting in His love. He was mighty to save her from loneliness and rejection; He rejoiced over Kelly with singing. The miracle of that particular morning was that God allowed Kelly to hear it.

There may be those like Thomas who'd doubt what they haven't yet experienced themselves, but Kelly knows what she heard. That morning, Kelly was awakened to the sound of a heavenly anthem. Angelic voices in beautiful harmonies stirred her from sleep, joyously announcing:

"Your husband is coming. Prepare for your husband. Prepare to be a bride."

As you can imagine, Kelly was overwhelmed. There was no mistaking the source of this message. She had been slumbering peacefully—not striving, not interacting with any human being—when suddenly, the windows of heaven opened up to her. There was no name this time, no timeline. She'd heard only that sweet musical leading to prepare for what was to come. It was a wonder that would be repeated many times. Kelly treasured the experience in her heart, and she went about responding to the call of it.

Prepare to Be a Bride

How does a woman prepare to be a bride? What does that process look like, specifically? For Kelly, the starting place was her heart. She began by asking the Lord to teach her everything He wanted her to learn. She asked Him to prepare her from the inside to be the kind of wife He wanted her to be. In faith, she prayed for the husband God would reveal to her at exactly the right time.

Kelly read about Esther's year of preparation before she was presented to the king. She began to use special oils and creams, beautifying herself for her husband-to-be like Esther did. As a way of toning her body, she started a regular walking regimen. Kelly's mother was a good cook, so she collected family recipes from her, and then developed her own culinary style. Money was tight, but Kelly knew it was time to say goodbye to the raggedly lingerie of her single life. Those worn gowns and granny panties had to go! Kelly replaced them with intimate apparel appropriate for the bride she believed she'd become.

Before long, Kelly was cast as the lead in a musical about—you guessed it—a bride. Yes, God really is in the details! So, even in the course of readying herself for this acting job, Kelly immersed herself in what it meant to become someone's wife. Since the play was a musical about a bride, Kelly briefly wondered if this role were the fulfillment of the musical annunciation she'd heard, but she continued to prepare for a real, live husband, even after the play's run came to a close.

Six months after her bridal preparation began, Kelly received an invitation to attend an awards ceremony. It was the kind of dressy affair that can be daunting for a woman to attend alone, so she was inclined to turn it down. However, when Kelly prayed about it, she heard what had become a familiar still, small voice say:

"Go, and I will bless you."

"Hmmm. What to wear?" Kelly thought on the evening of the awards. Though many would have chosen flashier attire, Kelly slipped into a feminine sweater dress. She had no idea of the blessing that awaited her. Neither did Jay.

Jay spotted Kelly immediately when she walked into the awards event in that soft off-white dress.

From across the room, Jay turned to a friend and said, *"Who is that?!"*

The way Jay tells it, he knew from the first moment he saw Kelly's face that she was The One for him. He quickly made his way over and introduced himself. Then, Jay stayed at Kelly's side for the rest of the evening, staking his claim by fending off the attentions of other men who noticed her. They became inseparable.

A month or two later, God moved upon Kelly and Jay simultaneously, each in different ways, while they were in separate rooms. The voice Kelly heard was quiet but clear:

"This is the man you've been praying for."

It was at that same moment that God did something profound inside Jay, in the other room. There are times words fail to express an experience and this may be one of them. But Jay says it was like God took his heart and pulled it out toward Kelly like a big rubber band or suspenders, and then snapped it back into his chest. Jay knew in that moment that he loved Kelly the way a man loves a woman he wants to be with for the rest of his life.

When they were together again later, Kelly looked deeply into Jay's eyes. The truth of what God had spoken settled into Kelly's heart. Jay was, indeed, the answer to her prayers.

After a moment of sheer wonder, she simply said, "It's you, isn't it?"

Jay returned Kelly's gaze in a way no other man had. "Yes. It's me," Jay replied.

Kelly and Jay didn't compare notes on their separate experiences, but both took steps of faith. Secretly, Jay asked Kelly's parents for her hand. While her mom and dad kept Jay's confidence, Kelly visited a fabric store and chose a special pattern for her wedding dress.

Soon after Kelly's parents gave him permission, Jay asked Kelly to be his bride. It was my privilege to read the Scripture as they were wed many years ago, and it has been my great joy to see their very happy and enduring marriage. God blessed Kelly with Jay, beyond her wildest imaginings. Jay is a prince among men and he has always treated Kelly like the princess that she is. They are perfectly suited for each other, just as their heavenly Father knew they would be.

The button on this story came long after Kelly and Jay were married. Kelly hadn't thought about the vision she'd had of that comfortable sort of guy, that picture she'd seen years prior to when she met Jay. Ages before, she had chalked the image up to wishful thinking, and it had never crossed Kelly's mind as she dated Jay.

But one day, as Kelly gazed into the eyes of her husband, that vision came flooding back to her in vivid detail. Jay's height, hair coloring, and beard were an exact match. Jay had even been a producer when they'd met, just as she'd supposed when she'd seen that long ago vision. Mostly, it was those shining eyes of Jay's that Kelly recognized, and it was the way she'd been so completely comfortable with Jay, right from the beginning.

Finally, Kelly knew that the vision she'd seen had been much more than an invention of a young woman's imagination. It had come from the only One who could have known so far in advance what would actually come to be. It had come from God.

Kelly had chosen Jay as The One.

She had chosen him of her own free will.

And yet it was a choice her omnipotent Lord had always seen coming.

Jay's eyes shone all the more as Kelly related the vision. They couldn't help smiling to think how God was so much bigger than their circuitous paths to the altar. Despite the mistakes they'd both made along the way, God had still found a way to guide them to each other.

Together, they thanked God for each and every relationship that didn't work out, and especially for this one that, with His help, did.

Ladies in Waiting

Over the course of this book, I've introduced you to a number of dear friends and family members. You've met Cheryl, Anna, Bethany, and Kelly—women who have believed God and have had been led to the altar in glorious ways. I've told you their stories to give you hope, especially those of you who have been waiting a long while. You've also met Rachel and Paula who, as of this writing, are still waiting and trusting in their heavenly Father. They wanted me to share their experiences so you'd know you are far from alone if you are still waiting, too.

Some men may read this book. Some married people may take a gander. But most will be single, part of a special sisterhood, a society of women who understand well how you feel.

Would you like to know a secret? The musical miracle that Kelly experienced on her bed that morning is also happening for you. That's right. You may not be able to hear it as Kelly did, but the Lord your God is singing over you, too. It's hard to imagine, isn't it? The Creator of the universe, the composer of your love story, sings for joy to think of all He is preparing for you, His beloved.

No matter how it may seem, you are not alone. He understands the human rejection you feel, and has chosen you as His own. No matter how lengthy the road, your God is there at your side, encouraging you onward. He longs to draw you out of the pit of despair, to dress you in white, and to fill your heart with love beyond measure.

Hang onto that promise, Daughter of the King. To do so is faith in one of its most exquisite expressions. It's a tender assurance that transcends any doubt over what is not yet seen, a trust that the very best will surely come to pass. It's a radiant bride, peacefully walking down the aisle of life, on the arm of her heavenly Father.

> *"For from old they have not heard nor perceived by ear, neither has the eye seen a God besides Thee, who acts in behalf of the one who waits for Him."*
>
> *Isaiah 64:4*

About the Author

Susan Rohrer is an honor graduate of James Madison University where she studied Art and Communications, and thereafter married in her native state of Virginia. A professional writer, producer, and director specializing in redemptive entertainment, Rohrer's credits in one or more of these capacities include: an adaptation of *God's Trombones;* 100 episodes of drama series *Another Life;* Humanitas Prize finalist & Emmy winner *Never Say Goodbye;* Emmy nominees *Terrible Things My Mother Told Me* and *The Emancipation of Lizzie Stern;* anthology *No Earthly Reason;* NAACP Image Award nominee *Mother's Day;* AWRT Public Service Award winner (for addressing the problem of high school sexual harassment) *Sexual Considerations;* comedy series *Sweet Valley High;* telefilms *Book of Days* and

Another Pretty Face; Emmy nominee & Humanitas Prize finalist *If I Die Before I Wake;* as well as Film Advisory Board & Christopher Award winner *About Sarah.* Rohrer is also the author of *The Holy Spirit: Amazing Power for Everyday People.*

> *"But whatever things were gain to me, those things I have counted as loss for the sake of Christ. More than that, I count all things to be loss in view of the surpassing value of knowing Christ Jesus my Lord...that I may know Him, and the power of His resurrection."*
>
> *Philippians 3:7–8a, 10a*

Other Books You May Enjoy:

THE HOLY SPIRIT:
Amazing Power for Everyday People
by Susan Rohrer

NEVER THE BRIDE: a novel
by Cheryl McKay & Rene Gutteridge

FINALLY THE BRIDE:
Finding Hope While Waiting
By Cheryl McKay

Made in the USA
San Bernardino, CA
06 February 2013